Deliverance For Christians
Level 1
Claiming Your Freedom in Christ
Combined Book and Workbook

By
Susan V. Fernandez
Artos Ministries: Deliverance For Christians
Lake Forest, California
www.DeliveranceForChristians.com

_____

Your Name

_____

Start Date

Deliverance For Christians Level 1
Claiming Your Freedom in Christ
Combined Book and Workbook

Written by Susan V. Fernandez
Manuscript prepared by Susan V. Fernandez
Cover Design by Rachel M. Dodson

ATTENTION:
Unless specified otherwise, Scriptures are used are from the
New American Standard Bible.

If Quotations are from the New American Standard Bible (1995
Updated Edition): "Scripture taken from the *NEW AMERICAN
STANDARD BIBLE®*, © Copyright 1960, 1962, 1963, 1968, 1971,
1972, 1973, 1975, 1977, 1995 by The Lockman Foundation
Used by permission." (www.Lockman.org)

If Quotations are from the New American Standard Bible (1977
Edition): "Scripture taken from the *NEW AMERICAN STANDARD
BIBLE®*, © Copyright 1960, 1962, 1963, 1968, 1971, 1972, 1973,
1975, 1977 by The Lockman Foundation
Used by permission." (www.Lockman.org)

Artos Ministries
25422 Trabuco Road, Suite 105-385
Lake Forest, CA 92630
Email: DeliveranceForChristians@cox.net
Website: www.DeliveranceForChristians.com

ISBN: ISBN-13: 978-0692902936

DEDICATION

To my dear parents Allan and Virginia, whose extreme generosity has allowed me to spend much of my life serving the Lord in whatever He has called me to do. Thank you, Mom and Dad! I love you! See you in Heaven!

To my not-of-this-world husband Charlie and our six children (David, Jonathan, Rachel, Rebekah, Angelique, and Shawn) and their amazing families.

To my earthly blood brothers Kent and David and their families who I love and appreciate more than words can say.

And to my dear brothers and sisters in Christ who have labored side-by-side with me and my family as we strive to obey the calling of The Great Commission in our little corner of this world.

I love you all!

Most of all, to my one and only Father God, Jesus Christ, and Holy Spirit – who give me all that I need to walk in Freedom in Christ.

Amen.

One final thought prior to your starting this book…

The Bible tells us In <u>Hebrews 4:14-16</u>: *"Therefore, since we have a great high priest who has passed through the heavens, Jesus the Son of God, let us hold fast our confession. For we do not have a high priest who cannot sympathize with our weaknesses, but One who has been tempted in all things as we are, yet without sin.* **Therefore let us draw near with confidence to the throne of grace, so that we may receive mercy and find grace to help in time of need.***"*

*This whole passage is extremely important for us, but <u>I especially want to point out the **location** from which we are to pray.</u>*

*I recently realized that I shout from earth to Heaven when I want to talk to God…instead of going to His throne room of grace as He tells us to – in order that I may speak with Him intimately - face-to-face. Jesus is also there as our Advocate. <u>I John 2:1</u> "My little children, I am writing these things to you so that you may not sin. And if anyone sins, we have an **Advocate** with the Father, Jesus Christ the righteous…"*

Please take a moment to allow this concept to fully sink into your being and then embrace it <u>every time you go to prayer</u> from now on. Pause. Go to the throne room by faith. And THEN begin your prayers, praises, and petitions as you speak intimately with your Father and His Son.

I believe that your relationship with God will change dramatically just by your being in the best location from which to speak to Him.

Thank You, Father!

TABLE OF CONTENTS

APPENDICES
IN ALPHABETICAL ORDER

NOTE FROM AUTHOR

VERY IMPORTANT! PLEASE READ!

Dear Reader,

I am going to be very honest and transparent with you right now. Except for the Bible, I rarely, if ever, read a book where I completely wholeheartedly agree with everything the author has written. Why is that?

- *Perhaps he has had different experiences in his life than I have had and therefore, he has learned something I have yet to learn.*
- *Or perhaps I am the one who has experienced different things than he has yet to learn, and I could actually teach him something too.*

We must keep in mind that the Bible is a living Book and thus the truth, knowledge, and wisdom that we comprehend will grow with us as we grow. Salvation is a lifelong experience of walking forward in Jesus' name and learning of His ways, His commands, His love…everything about Him and what He has for us.

Because it is a lifelong process, had I written a book about deliverance when I was in my twenties, it would have undoubtedly looked very different from the book I have written today – due to my own growth in learning about God and His ways.

All to say, as you read this book, glean from it what makes sense to you now.

If you are able to agree with everything, then Praise God! But if you do not agree or maybe just do not fully understand, please do not stop reading! Keep going! Because at the very least you will learn things that you did not know before.

Bottom line? Please read the entire book from front to back. Underline, circle, and write in it. Make it yours! This is best used as a journal for you – to chart your own personal walk towards freedom. Everyone's journey will look different, but it will lead us all to the same place - Freedom in Christ!

If you find that you do not understand or do not agree with something, mark it and then pray about it. Ask the Lord to explain it to you in words that will make sense to you personally. And then, of course, you are always welcome to email us with questions as well.

The Holy Spirit is all over this book. In fact, He wrote it! So please...go to the One who created you and seek His help in understanding your walk to freedom. Above all - DO NOT GIVE UP and DO NOT LOOK BACK. Determine within yourself to DO WHATEVER IT TAKES to obtain the Freedom Christ died for – JUST FOR YOU!

It is with great excitement and anticipation that I present to you:
Deliverance For Christians Level 1: Claiming Your Freedom in Christ

With God's Love For You,

Sue Fernandez

INTRODUCTION
How It All Began

Over the past 35 years, the Lord has given me tool after tool to use in my "spiritual tool belt" to help carry out one of the callings He has given me – to help people obtain personal freedom in Christ. My primary motivational spiritual gift is exhortation, which is the desire to help those in the Body of Christ to grow in their relationships with the Lord Jesus Christ. That is my passion. That is what I was created to do. And that is why I am writing this book - so that you, too, can learn not only how to grow in your relationship with the Lord, but to also fully claim the freedom He died on the cross to give you.

Many years ago, even as a child in first grade, my gifting was generally exhibited in encouraging others. I loved helping the most down-and-out kids at school, always favoring the underdog. It was in my nature & character to want to help those who truly needed it.

Later in my twenties, the Lord moved me into a more serious form of encouraging the down-and-out when I began working with recovering drug and alcohol addicts. I counseled and helped them prepare for finding work and taught them what they needed to know academically in order to obtain their General Equivalency Diploma. Some of those I worked with were grown men who had worked in factories their entire lives. When the factories closed down, and men were laid off, many of those men were unemployable because they had never learned how to read! I loved this job because I was able to combine the practical with the spiritual to help people get back on their feet again. But I soon realized these people I worked with had some problems that I, as a young 23-year-old, was not fully qualified to offer counsel on.

The one case that catapulted me into obtaining more training was a young female client who told me her story of being perpetually raped throughout her entire life. It first started with her father who incestuously molested her throughout her childhood. This eventually drove her into a mental institution. There, staff and patients further sexually molested her, until finally she met a fellow patient whom, because he was soon to be released, she decided to marry, so that she could leave the institution with him. It was the only thing she could think to do to get out of that hellish place. Unfortunately, this man that she married also continued raping her multiple times a day until she was finally able to run away from him. She turned to the streets, drugs and alcohol, and eventually ended up in the organization for which I worked.

It was through meeting this woman as part of my caseload that I realized it would be beneficial for me to obtain more tools to help people who had gone through dire situations such as these. I began classes at a local seminary where I learned some valuable information as a "nouthetic" counselor, thereby gaining a greater understanding of how to help people. (*Nouthetic counseling* in a nutshell is lay members of The Church counseling others using the Bible and the guidance of the Holy Spirit to help people put into practice what the Word of God teaches.

That was the beginning of my journey into officially becoming a lay counselor, and over the years, I continued to counsel many others - encouraging them in their walks with the Lord. This has gone on now for many years, never with pay, but always with a heart of love for God and for His people.

In about the year 2000, the Lord began to step things up for my husband and me during a period when my husband was laid off from work. It was clearly a God thing. Through various circumstances, an opportunity came along for us to become missionaries to Russia, which had just recently been set free from communism. We prayed about it and decided to accept the calling.

We began preparations, which included putting our house on the market for sale and taking a short trip to Russia to assess our soon-to-be new home. From the moment we stepped onto Russian soil until the moment we left, we were overcome by the oppressive darkness that reigned there. It was an effort just to put one foot in front of the other, so heavy was the darkness. Within hours of landing, both my husband and I were in tears, wondering if we really had what it would take to walk out this calling. It would require us to sell everything and move our four small children to this Godless country, with the oppressive forces being beyond anything most people from the U.S. could even imagine.

Upon returning back to the States, we decided after much prayer and out of sheer obedience to the Lord, to continue pursuing our move to Moscow. We also decided that it was time to start praying for Moscow in preparation for the work we would do there. It was this decision that then moved us into a whole new dimension of life we had never experienced before. We began a seven-day fast for the purpose of binding the principalities and powers of Moscow over the area where we would be serving. Towards the end of those seven days, it was clear that something was happening in the spiritual realm far beyond anything we had anticipated.

Our children and we began hearing our names called. We would turn around to see who was calling to us, and no one would be there. Some of us felt fear. Others had contention. At one point, my husband even felt suicidal and actually got a gun out! He quickly snapped to attention, realizing something was very wrong. We had no idea what was going on, but immediately we called the family together (our four children at ages 8, 9, 10, and 11) to talk about what was happening. As we compared stories of the things each of us had been experiencing, we realized these things were actually demonic. Even as we were talking, our oldest son started shaking, covered his eyes, and pointed to the doorway. When he was finally able to speak, with fear and trembling he reported that there was a huge demonic figure standing at least 12 feet tall, leaning down and peering through the doorway of our vaulted ceiling room. As do many that first encounter the dark side of the spiritual realm, we fell to our knees and began to pray. My husband broke out in Holy Spirit tongues, commanding whatever it was to leave.

Since we had already learned about and taken care of the spiritual cleansing of our home in the years prior to this time (something you will learn more about in this book), this dark figure (whatever it was) did not have license to be there. We believe it was probably sent to scope us out because of our prayer and fasting against the satanic forces in Moscow. Thankfully it left our home fairly quickly, but it became obvious to us that we were way out of our league in our knowledge and understanding of how to deal with things of this nature. Thus began our journey into the spiritual world of conflict, where Satan tries to steal souls away from God.

As Christians, we all somewhat know there is an unseen battle going on around us, but most of us have been taught, *"If we focus on God and ignore the enemy, he will leave us alone."* We soon learned this was a lie from hell meant to take us to a place of complacency and ignorance, and that we needed to step up our game if we were ever going to have any kind of success in taking the gospel into a foreign, majorly oppressed land like Russia. It was not long before we began to realize that we also had a calling to spiritual warfare and that we needed to intensify our study on this subject, since we had very little knowledge of how to fight against the darkness of the enemy that wanted to come against us to stop us.

Over the next several years, we continued to increase in knowledge and understanding of the spiritual realm and we learned how to operate with the forces of God against the forces of evil. It has not been an easy path, because anytime one takes an offensive posture towards the enemy, there is going to be counterattack. Naturally, the enemy is not going to just watch us attack. He will fight back too. It is literally a battle! And the enemy's retaliation usually, if not always, comes in the areas where we are the weakest and the most vulnerable.

On this path, as we battled with evil time and time again, we suffered the loss of many friendships, including relationships with relatives. We endured the loss of reputation and a lack of success. But through it all, we continued to persevere. We did not try to avoid or go around counterattacks. And we definitely did not retreat from them. We continued to push right straight through the middle of each and every attack. The result? Our spiritual muscles grew stronger and stronger, and we became better equipped to go to battle with the authority, power, and knowledge that God has given to all true Sons and Daughters of God through our Savior and Lord Jesus Christ.

Is Spiritual Warfare for every Christian? Yes, to a certain extent, it is. The Bible tells us in <u>Ephesians 6:10-17</u>, *"Finally, be strong in the Lord and in the strength of His might. Put on the full armor of God, so that you will be able to stand firm against the schemes of the devil. For our struggle is not against flesh and blood, but against the rulers, against the powers, against the world forces of this darkness, against the spiritual forces of wickedness in the heavenly places. Therefore, take up the full armor of God, so that you will be able to resist in the evil day, and having done everything, to stand firm. Stand firm therefore, having girded your loins with truth, and having put on the breastplate of righteousness, and having shod your feet with the preparation of the gospel of peace; in addition to all, taking up the shield of faith with which you will be able to extinguish all the flaming arrows of the evil one. And take the helmet of salvation, and the sword of the Spirit, which is the Word of God. With all prayer and petition pray at all times in the Spirit, and with this in view, be on the alert with all perseverance and petition for all the saints, and pray on my behalf, that utterance may be given to me in the opening of my mouth, to make known with boldness the mystery of the gospel, for which I am an ambassador in chains; that in proclaiming it I may speak boldly, as I ought to speak."*

Are some of us called to higher levels of warfare? Yes, probably so.

What is the determining factor of whether you are called to a higher level of spiritual warfare or not? From our experience, there are three things: Desire, Perseverance, and Stamina. All three are required to attain a higher ranking in the army of God at a spiritual warfare level. It is not for the weak or the faint of heart. The Bible tells us we must count the cost, because we need to be willing to not only risk our own lives but also the lives of our loved ones. It seems that very few are willing to do this. <u>Matthew 22:14</u> *"For many are called, but few are chosen."*

Russia never ended up happening for us. The Lord later told us that our experience had been an Abraham/Isaac test (<u>Genesis 22</u>) to see if we would be willing to give up everything in order to go to the mission field. The answer was, "*Yes!*" We had already proven this by selling or donating almost everything we owned. The only thing that had stood between Russia and us was selling or renting out our house. We had put our "Isaac" on the altar and just as it was about to be "consumed as a sacrifice," the Lord said, "*STOP! You are not to go. This was a test. You have passed. Now I will show you what you are to do instead.*"

The "instead" started as a ministry that began with single parents...then evolved to single moms and their children...and then to all people of all ages. As a group of believers, we prayed together, we studied the Bible together, we had a home church together, and we had fellowship together. Through all of this, the underlying theme for our family has always come back to the fact that we have been called to spiritual warfare.

As we have delved deeper into using what we have learned in order to battle the forces of darkness, we have found new ways of helping True Children of God get free of the darkness that surrounds them. This is the darkness that most have no idea they even have, because they have learned to live with it! Are these True Christ-Followers saved and going to Heaven? Most of them are! But many and even most of them have not yet been cleansed and healed from the past ongoing defilement of the enemy by way of the strongholds on their souls. (You will learn more about strongholds in this book.) As time has progressed, the Lord has been faithful to give us more and more tools to help people claim personal Freedom in Christ.

Now after many years of seasoning in the spiritual warfare and deliverance realms, we have seen hundreds of Brothers and Sisters in Christ claim the freedom that Jesus died for! We hope and pray that you will find that freedom too, as you go through this workbook and put to action the God-given wisdom and knowledge contained within it. All honor and praise go to You, Lord Jesus Christ of Nazareth!

Sue Fernandez

PURPOSE OF THIS BOOK

For many years, I have met with people on an individual basis to help them claim their Freedom in Christ. Generally, this process takes the time of about six two-hour sessions, with tune-up appointments once or twice a year. As you can imagine, this can be time-consuming - and as my waiting list became longer and longer, I soon realized that with so few deliverance ministers - and deliverance being a need that every Child of God has - the members of the Body of Christ will have a hard time all being set fully free with the one-on-one method only. So my prayer became, *"Lord, we need a Plan B."*

Many books have been written about deliverance and while many are excellent sources of information, they often only touch the surface of what deliverance really needs to look like at a practical hands-on and, most importantly, personal level. There are a number of programs that claim to do deliverance on people, but many of them only scratch the surface of deliverance. Often there is a renouncing of this and a renouncing of that, but the deliverance is not fully personalized to the individual. As a result, there is often more damage done than good, because the individual will think he has been set free - when in reality he has only just begun. And an individual who is partly free and partly demonized cannot always tell which-voice-is-which in the spiritual realm, and because of this, a lot of damage can be done - not only within himself but also to his family and friends - and even to his church.

THERE ARE NO QUICK DELIVERANCE PROGRAMS. Deliverance is a layered process. I often tell people – it is like gold that is being refined. It is heated up. The top layer of impurities is scraped off, and then the gold is heated more. At that point, more impurities float up. Those need to be scraped off. This process needs to continue on until the gold has been purified. So it is with deliverance. It is not a once-and-done process, and in fact it is something that we will return to time and again throughout our lives when new incidents come up that require our attention, in order for us to be set free of the enemy's lies which are attached to the memory strongholds in our minds.

Some churches and parachurch organizations will cast out demons/spirits from people on the spot. Someone will discern, for instance, that a sister has a spirit of lust. So, they will pray over her to cast out the spirit of lust. And that spirit MAY even leave her. But there are two problems that we frequently see. First of all, they do not tell the demon where to go, so if the demon came out, it could have easily entered someone standing nearby (including a child), if that "someone" had a stronghold for the demon to attach to. And secondly, if that sister had an enemy stronghold that was not dealt with at the root level of it, there is an almost certain likelihood that the demon will come back and reattach because of the "license" she still has on her soul – and, even worse, it may bring other demons with it! (Matthew 12:43-45) Because of this, I do NOT recommend your allowing anyone to casually cast demons out of you, no matter how well intended he may be. If he is just doing it on the spot and has no intention of sitting down with you later to find out how and why the demons got there to begin with, then I would wait until you can work with someone who is willing to do that – and knows how to help you at a deeper level. From what I have seen, there are at least two different motivations for the quick method of casting out demons. One is sheer ignorance of what is really involved. (Many Christians think that boldness is all that is needed.) The second is that some people enjoy the drama and the sensationalism of dealing with the demonic.

Here is the thing. Yes, we do need a certain amount of boldness, and at times there is drama that goes with it, if the demonic manifest. But if we do not deal with the demonic from a place of understanding, wisdom, and knowledge, then we are like a small child with a gun – shooting at anything that moves. This can be extremely dangerous for anyone in the vicinity. The verse comes to mind: *"My people are destroyed for lack of knowledge."* Hosea 4:6 And I believe this is true when it comes to deliverance. If you do not really know what you are doing, then you must be extremely careful. The Holy Spirit will sometimes reveal something that needs to be dealt with but be sure to ask Him for the wisdom on what steps of action are to be taken. And then always follow up with someone who is experienced in these matters, for confirmation that everything that needed to be done was done by you. We may, at times, be dealing with a crisis situation, but the follow-up health plan, figuratively speaking, will need more attention and implementation. (You will understand more about this as you continue reading through this book.)

All of this said, we now come to the primary reason for this book. We believe that every Child of God can work together with the Holy Spirit to help set a friend, relative, and/or even himself - free in Christ. I pray that this workbook will give you the information you need to become knowledgeable about the dark side and give you the beginning level of tools with which to fight against the enemy for your own personal freedom. After you have gained your own freedom, you will then be able to help others gain their freedom! It is a wonderful process and a wonderful calling - to help people receive the full freedom that Jesus died for!

WHAT IS DELIVERANCE?

First of all, let me state here in the beginning that it is highly recommended that you read through this entire book before you begin working on your own personal deliverance. Every facet is used in each step of the process, and it will be most helpful to you if you have an overall idea of what all the processes are and what the terms mean before you actually dive into doing it for yourself. If at any time you have questions about anything contained in this book, please visit the website and look at the FAQ page and/or email us your question, so that we can help to clarify.
Website: www.deliveranceforchristians.com

Deliverance is a broad term that has a number of components to it. The concept of deliverance is taken from the Greek word *soteria* which means DELIVERANCE, SALVATION. Acts 4:12 *"And there is salvation (soteria) in no one else; for there is no other name under heaven that has been given among men by which we must be saved."* The Bible in Philippians 4:12 speaks about working out our own salvation (*soteria*) with fear and trembling. So, at the point that we repent (repentance being very key!) of our sins and ask Jesus to take control of our lives, we cross the line into a personal relationship with Jesus Christ and look forward to eternal life in Heaven. Many Christians think that at that point all demonic forces flee, and the Christian has only then to follow the commands of Christ in the Bible to lead a successful life in Him. (Note: *Soteria* is used 45 times in the New Testament.)

I personally spent a good 40 to 45 years doing what I now call *"muscling my way through Christianity."* With God's grace and sheer willpower, I was able to fairly successfully live a Christian life, wherein my sins were not obvious to the casual observer. But about that time, the impact of what the Bible really says hit me hard. *"If the Son sets you free, you will be free indeed."* John 8:36 And *"I came to give you life and give it to you abundantly."* John 10:10 And lastly, *"My burden is light."* Matthew 11:30 At one point, these things really sank into me and I began to reason…*"If Jesus' burden is light, then I must be doing something wrong!"*

In my effort to always be working in a positive direction on my salvation transformation, I recalled a teaching I had learned in the not-too-distant past about strongholds and how we can actually ask the Lord to break them off. I remembered seeing a picture that showed how the enemy builds fortresses (strongholds) on our souls and operates from these positions of legal right by telling us lies and deceiving us into thinking things about ourselves and/or about others that are false. (See II Corinthians 10:3-5.)

One day as I was working in my kitchen I thought, "*Hmmm. What can it hurt to try to break off as strongholds some of the memories of my past that come up to haunt me at times…*" So, I said a short prayer. "*Father, in Jesus name, I ask that You take back the ground that was given to the enemy when I…*(and I cited something from my past). *I ask that You break that stronghold from my soul.*" I repeated this for a couple of things as they came to mind from my past. Within a few days, I noticed a very subtle but distinct difference in the way I felt. There was a greater sense of peace. I felt calmer. It was at that point, that I became very interested in the fact that this sheer and very simple act of faith (asking the Lord to take back ground and break the strongholds) seemed to be doing something invisible to my soul that was making me feel much better and much freer! (Again let me say that this was happening after decades of my having been a Child of God who had actively been "*working out my own salvation with fear and trembling.*")

From that time on, I launched into learning more about strongholds, what causes them, how the enemy uses them, and how to get rid of them. Soon after that, I began incorporating this information into my counseling sessions. That was about 25 years ago.

A few years later was our call to Russia and then we experienced the steps that led us to moving more into the satanic dark realm from the point of Spiritual Warfare. Things progressed from then on, with the Lord putting piece after piece after piece of the deliverance puzzle together for us, until what developed were powerful and mighty tools of God to rout the enemy out of lives and set people free! God is good!

So in a nutshell, deliverance involves getting rid of the legal right that the enemy has to our homes and our lives, including our souls (which includes our mind, will, and emotions). It also includes deep inner healing, as needed. It includes forgiving others by the grace of God. It includes recognizing the lies of the enemy and learning what it is that God has to say in His Word about us - and the ways we should live. It includes learning how to walk out His commands and promises to us in the ways He has designed for us. And last but not least (and this is usually only about 10% of the overall process of deliverance), it includes the breaking off and/or out of any demons that have had license to our souls through the strongholds that were built there by the enemy.

Many people, when they hear the word "deliverance," immediately picture some of the more sordid things we have all seen in the media with a lot of drama, yelling, and manifestations of demons – and, quite frankly, most people do not want to go there. Who can blame them? In my experience, however, if the license is dealt with first and removed, the soul is cleansed and healed, and instruction is given on walking out God's truth, then the demonic will begin to dissipate from the person, often even before being called on to do so! The reason for this is that there is no longer anything they have to hold onto in that cleansed soul. Very rarely (5% of the time) do demons fight from releasing and end up manifesting in a dramatic way. Usually this happens mostly when there is deep entrenchment of iniquity in the family line and thereby generational license that is deeply rooted. This is often the case where there has been generational idol worship and false religions such as witchcraft, Santeria, Freemasonry, etc. (You will learn more about this in the material to come.)

Again, my greatest desire is to see every Christian Brother and Sister claim his or her Freedom in Christ. It makes living together in unity so much more doable, because no longer are we bumping up against one another's sensitive spots where lies and deceit have attached to past wounds...which causes us to not trust one another…which causes us to be so caught up in our own issues that we cannot get our eyes off of ourselves long enough to help someone else…which causes us to retaliate with pain and rejection rather than understanding and forgiveness. The Body of Christ is in a HUGE mess - but not for long! Because many others and I are understanding the need for deliverance and saying, "*Enough is enough! Now is the time for us to rise up…get free in Christ…operate from hearts of love…and win souls - because others are watching us and when we are able to operate in freedom, they will want what we have found in Him!*"

CHRISTIAN ETHICS IN DELIVERANCE & COUNSELING

As you go through the following material in this workbook, you will be embarking on a wonderful journey of claiming your Freedom in Christ. You will learn many things that the average Christian has never heard before. Unfortunately, we live in a church age that is very Nicolaitan in nature, meaning – the pastor speaks - and you listen. Many churches do not teach the saints with the goal of equipping them to be individually powerful and authoritative in the name of Jesus Christ. There is little chance for you to learn what your gifts are or how to use them, and rarely are you given the opportunity to use them should you actually happen to know what they are (unless, of course, you are a pastor, teach Sunday school, or are an administrator, usher, or deacon).

As Christians, we are also taught - or at least surmise from what we are taught or not taught, as the case often is: *If we just accept Christ as our Savior and ignore the enemy, the enemy will go away.*

How like Satan to propagate this lie in the church today. It makes his job so much easier! When he is not recognized as the instigator of torment and heartbreak in our lives, then we blame others or ourselves for our situations! We remain inwardly focused trying to figure out our own problems. Meanwhile the lost are passing us by every day and we have no strength or knowledge to help them, because we cannot even figure out what to do in our own lives!

Our number one goal after salvation, baptism in water, and baptism in the Holy Spirit should be to claim our full Freedom in Christ through the process we call deliverance - meaning *"getting free from the clutches of the enemy in our lives."* The Bible tells us in John 8:36 *"For if the Son makes you free, you will be free indeed."* It is by His blood that this becomes possible. Once you have claimed your own freedom, you will then be better able to share with others how to obtain their freedom as well.

However, even with this Godly goal in mind, we must be sensitive to how and when we talk to others about the things we are learning. We want to be careful that we do not turn people off before we even get started. This is not what any of us wants. Know that you will have found POWERFUL tools to claim your Freedom in Christ. Yet, you do not want to chase people away because you are heavy-handed in explaining to someone (for instance) that *Hello Kitty* can bring a spirit of lust. Try to meet people where they are. If they ask questions and are curious, then you know you can go further with them. But if they look at you like you are crazy, plant a few seeds and then close out the conversation and pray for them until they are ready to hear more. Oftentimes they will actually come back to you after you have planted some seeds, the Lord has watered them, and they have become a little more comfortable with the information. Remember: Very few of today's churches teach about the spiritual realm. So it often takes a while for people to switch gears and be able to receive the truths you have gained.

Also, remember that the Lord tells us that we are to be wise and harmless. This means we must be led by and speak by His Holy Spirit at all times and not just blurt things out, even if they are truths. Please keep in mind that opinions do not count for anything! When you speak, speak only what you know is in alignment with our Heavenly Father's heart and Word.

So in talking to others about what you have learned, a starting point I like to recommend is to talk about memory strongholds. Most people (even atheists I have spoken with) can relate to the idea of having strongholds through emotional wounding, generational iniquities, and/or sin. This is my own personal approach - even now after so many years of helping people receive their Freedom in Christ. There are close friends I have who I do not even bring up the subject of deliverance with, because I know they would not be accepting of it right now. Do I pray for them and watch for an opportunity to speak to them about it? Absolutely! Have I crossed them off my list? No way! I am just waiting for God's timing, which I remind myself - is perfect.

Please Remember: *Living out your own freedom in Christ will make more of an impact on your loved ones than any words you could ever speak!* People WILL notice changes in you - and that alone will cause them to be drawn to you more and more. Earn the right to be heard by living out your freedom! When they start making comments about noticing changes in you, give them some examples from your own personal testimony of how the Lord set you free from memory strongholds or other things. When we focus on sharing what God has done in our lives, rather than trying to enlighten the other person of what it is THEY need, we will get a lot further in giving them an understanding of what we are talking about. Remember: Jesus often used parables to teach people, because people love stories! So use some of your own stories to plant seeds of curiosity and interest in the lives of the people you meet. After doing that, be sure they have your contact info and then pray for them. You will be surprised at how many will contact you down the road, after the Lord has had some time to work with those seeds you planted.

Besides the Good News of the gift of salvation through the blood of Jesus Christ, you have the best news in the world for people! Never be ashamed of it. Never cower down from it. Live it and live it to the fullest! With your freedom, let your Almighty God and Father live in and through you to others. I guarantee – they will notice!

PERSONAL PROGRESS RECORD

Name: Age: Start Date:

Salvation (Repentance) (See Appendix)   Yes   No   Date:

Water Baptism (See Appendix)   Yes   No   Date:

Holy Spirit Baptism (See Appendix)   Yes   No   Date:

Tongues (See Appendix)   Yes   No   Date

Spiritual Covering (See Appendix)   Yes   No   Who:

List your Spiritual Gifts. (If you do not know what your gifts are, see website www.DeliveranceForChristians.com for a Spiritual Gifts Assessment._____

Sin Memory Strongholds Broken   Yes   Date:

Emotional Memory Strongholds Broken   Yes   Date:

Forgiveness Granted   Yes   Date:

Family History Assessed   Yes   Date:

Repent for Generational Iniquities & Cords Cut   Yes   Date:

Word Curses/Spells Broken   Yes   Date:

Home Cleansed of Strongholds   Yes   Date:

Lust Repented For   Yes   Date:

Soul Ties Severed   Yes   Date:

Abortion Healing (Minister aide recommended)   Yes   Date:

Demons Removed   Yes   Date:

OVERVIEW OF WHAT IS COVERED

Remember to read through the entire workbook before you begin working on your own personal deliverance. Every facet is used in each step of the process, and it will be most helpful to you if you have an overall idea of what all the processes are and what the terms mean before you actually dive into doing it for yourself. Contact us with questions: DeliveranceForChristians@cox.net

Strongholds of the Soul: *Identifying and Breaking Off Root Sin & Emotional Memory Strongholds of the Enemy From Your Soul*

Forgiveness: *Learning the Secrets to Giving & Receiving Forgiveness*

Generational Iniquities: *Identifying, Repenting For, and Severing the Cords of Generational Sins, Transgressions, and Iniquities*

Curses and Spells: *Identifying and Breaking Off Curses/Spells You Did Not Realize Were Affecting You*

Strongholds of the Home: *Identifying and Breaking Off Strong-holds of the Enemy in Your Home*

Demonic Forces: *Identifying and Dealing With Demonic Forces That Are Affecting Your Life*

Soul Ties: *Identifying and Severing Unhealthy Soul Ties in a Healthy Way*

Lust: *Identifying and Breaking Off Lust and Its Manifestations in Your Life*

Abortion: *Ministering Healing to Those Who Have Participated in Abortion*

Appendices: *Various teachings designed as tools to not only help you personally, but also to help you help others as you disciple them in their walks with Jesus Christ.*

RECOMMENDED PRE-SESSION PRAYER

It is strongly recommended that the underlined portion of the prayer below be said at any time you are talking about the Lord (especially in public places) and generally anytime you are studying about (reading, internet, etc.) or acting in the mode of deliverance, spiritual warfare, and/or strategizing against the enemy. This is hands-down the most powerful tool we have used to significantly decrease enemy counterattack. It is a good habit to say this prayer at the beginning of each and every day.

Prior to all sessions of deliverance (including your own on yourself), we recommend adding in the rest of the prayer (not underlined) as a way to intentionally set up the spiritual realm for the Holy Spirit to move in your session, without interference from the enemy. After you set yourself up in the spiritual realm, be sure to have extra paper or even a notebook on hand to record progress, visions, etc. obtained during the deliverance process.

PRAYER OF ISOLATION FROM THE ENEMY

Father, in Jesus' name, I ask that You surround us with Your Holy Spirit and put us in complete isolation from the enemy throughout this day, so that nothing we say or do can be perceived by any force of the enemy.

I ask that You bind and cut off all outside forces of the enemy from the highest to the lowest levels and bind any forces of the enemy within our area of jurisdiction *until called upon to release. We especially ask that You bind all spirits of confusion, all familiar spirits masquerading as the Holy Spirit, and all spirits of fear.*

Guide us by Your Holy Spirit and lead us to the revelation, truth, wisdom, understanding, and knowledge that we need, in order to set (Name of Person) *free today. We call into existence the total freedom of* (Name of Person)*, the freedom that Jesus died for on the cross at Calvary. In Jesus' name, Amen.*

ARE YOU TRULY SAVED, OR HAVE YOU ONLY SAID, "THE SINNER'S PRAYER"?

In the Book of Revelation Jesus tells us numerous times, *"He who has an ear, let him hear what the Spirit says to the churches."* We are going through a period of time right now where the Spirit is saying, "Wake up! The time of Jesus' return is near! Ephesians 5:14 Get back to your first love! (Revelation 2:4) Stop being lukewarm!" Revelation 3:15-16

Why is He saying these and many other similar such things?

Because over the many centuries since the church of the disciples of Jesus Christ first began in Acts, the gospel message has been watered down, the truth of God's Word has been forgotten, and we have given way to the Nicolaitan form of "doing church" in a cookie-cutter format (worship-announcements-sermon-worship-dismiss). Over time we have even found a way to give people salvation – or so we think. All they need to do is "Say *The Sinner's Prayer*" and they are good to go! On their way to Heaven! Or are they?

What did Jesus say when He began His ministry on earth? He said, very simply, *"Repent. For the Kingdom of Heaven is at hand."* Matthew 4:17

Many, if not most, of today's churches have forgotten one of the most important parts of salvation. REPENTANCE! Often repentance is not even mentioned! What we hear far more often are things like: God loves you! Jesus will make your life brand new! Receive Christ today! Accept Jesus as your Savior!

And while these things are ALL true, we are missing some of the other very key truths of God's Word. We are not told that while we think we are basically "good people" - in actuality, Jesus says we are "wretched and miserable and poor and blind and naked"! Revelation 3:17 Or that there is "none righteous – no not one!" Romans 3:10 Or that after we are truly saved, that a brother or sister in Christ will be walking alongside of us, discipling us and helping us to learn about and then grow in the ways of our Savior! Matthew 28:1s

I bring this up because it is possible that while you may have: said "The Sinner's Prayer," gone forward at a church service, and/or even gotten water baptized – you may not truly be saved.

"How would I know?" you ask.

Jesus says very clearly that His followers will be known by the fruits of His Spirit in their lives. Those fruits are: love, joy, peace, patience, kindness, goodness, faithful-ness, gentleness, and self-control. Galatians 5:22-23 And conversely, if you have not truly been saved, you will likely be finding more of the deeds of the flesh operating in your life such as: immorality, impurity, sensuality, idolatry, sorcery, enmities, strife, jealousy, outbursts of anger, disputes, dissensions, factions, envying, drunkenness, carousing, and things like these. Galatians 5:19-21

What True Sons and Daughters of Jesus Christ must understand is that salvation is a supernatural experience. It is never something that we can impart on someone by their simply saying a formatted prayer. Believing in God is not enough! The Bible tells us in James 2:19 *"You believe that God is one. You do well; the demons also believe, and shudder."* Believing is a start, but there is more.

God's promise of true salvation requires something of us. He says in Jeremiah 29:13-14 " ***'You will seek Me and find Me when you search for Me with all your heart. I will be found by you,' declares the LORD…"***

Your true salvation is dependent on only two beings. You. And God. If you will seek after Him with all of your heart, truly wanting to know that He exists…that He is real…that He loves you and cares about you…then you will find Him - because He will show Himself to you!

If you have never done this and never had this kind of encounter with the One True and Living God, I would encourage you to stop right here and tell Him that you want this with Him. That you want to seek after Him with your whole heart and that as you do that, ask Him to show you Himself – so that you will know, without a doubt, that He is God and that He is worthy of your full trust and surrender to Him.

Pray that prayer in your own words and then as you feel ready after that, continue on with this book/workbook. Because in the process of all of this, He is going to show Himself to you in a way that you never even dreamed would be possible. You will start a love relationship with Him that is beyond anything you could even think to ask for! Ephesians 4:20

If you are ready for this journey, I highly recommend you get a Bible that you can write in. Almost all of the verses used in this book are from the New American Standard version of the Bible. I use this version because it is considered to be the most accurate version to the Hebrew and Greek meanings of the words used. But other decent versions are The King James Bible, The New King James Bible, or the English Standard Version. And I actually recommend you get two Bibles if you are able to afford them. One to write all over, taking notes, underlying, and highlighting as the Holy Spirit teaches you things. And then one Bible to have just to read and let the Lord speak to you giving you rhemas. (Rhemas are specific words given to you by God – that are just for you. Words that build you up, correct you, instruct you, etc.)

If you are a new believer, or even if you have been a true believer but have never done this, I recommend that you read from the beginning of the New Testament (which starts with the book of Matthew) all the way through to the last book which is Revelation. In this way, you will learn all about Jesus, his followers, and those who did not follow Him. You will even learn about some who said they followed Him, but when they were tested, we find out that they were not true followers after all. They were counterfeit followers!

Yes, the Word of God makes for very good reading!

When you are ready then, let us move forward into helping you now gain the freedom Christ promises you - His son or daughter.

WHAT ARE ENEMY STRONGHOLDS?

"For though we walk in the flesh, we do not war according to the flesh, for the weapons of our warfare are not of the flesh, but divinely powerful for the destruction of fortresses (strongholds). We are destroying speculations and every lofty thing raised up against the knowledge of God, and we are taking every thought captive to the obedience of Christ..." <u>II Corinthians 10:3-6</u>

- Free Dictionary: **Stronghold** = A fortified place or a fortress.[1]

- Strong's Concordance defines it this way. **Stronghold** (Noun, Greek 3794 ochyrōmaton) is: A fortress, strong defense, stronghold.[2]

- The definition I personally use for enemy strongholds is:

  A Satanic Stronghold is a place of operation in the spiritual realm - started by a MEMORY, a SIN, or a GENERATIONAL INIQUITY - where the enemy can gain ground (or license) on one's soul for evil purposes.

  o Enemy strongholds are a place of defense for the devil and his minions, where demonic or sinful activity is actually defended within us by our own sympathetic thoughts toward evil. We usually do not realize this is the case. We do not see that we are actually coming into agreement with the enemy (giving him "license") by believing his lies and distortions.

  o **License** is *official or legal permission to do or own a specified thing.*

---

[1] Free Dictionary: https://www.thefreedictionary.com/stronghold
[2] Bible Hub (Strong's Lexicon): https://biblehub.com/parallel/2_corinthians/10-4.htm

WHERE IS AN ENEMY STRONGHOLD?

An enemy stronghold is built on the soul.

A **STRONGHOLD** is built on the SOUL

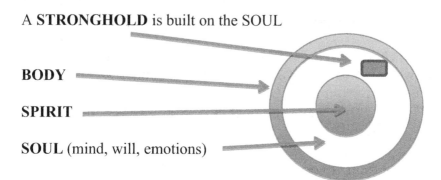

BODY

SPIRIT

SOUL (mind, will, emotions)

A STRONGHOLD in the physical realm gives us an idea of what a STRONGHOLD in the spiritual realm may look like - even though we cannot actually see it in the spiritual realm. A stronghold is a fortified place of operation where the enemy has been able to use weapons of warfare to gain control of someone else's property. So it is in the spiritual realm. The weapons of warfare used by the enemy are lies, deceit, and the actions of his own forces of darkness. With these things, he is able control us through our minds or emotions and/or by convincing us that he is also able to control our wills (although in reality this is not possible*). It becomes a base of operation for Satan. But he does not stop there. He will continue to build other strongholds on our souls in the same way by using whatever "license" we knowingly or unknowingly give him to do so. [*God has chosen to not give Himself the option to control our wills, so that we must make our OWN CHOICE to love and follow Him – or not. Therefore, I personally do not believe He gives Satan that option either - to be able to control our wills. Again, it is our choice whose voice we obey – or not.]

WHAT DOES THE ENEMY WANT FROM ME?

- He wants to steal from you. John 10:10

- He wants to destroy you. John 10:10

- He wants to kill you. John 10:10

WHAT DOES JESUS WANT FOR ME?

- He wants you to have freedom! John 8:36

- He wants you to have an abundant life! John 10:10

- He wants you to have a future and a hope! Jeremiah 29:11

- He wants to be your stronghold and your deliverer. Psalm 144:1-2

IMPORTANT NOTE

*Let me take a moment here to say that there are also **GODLY STRONGHOLDS** and they are all founded in our One True God. Deliverance For Christians Level 2 will teach you how to walk out your freedom in Christ and with the Holy Spirit's help – to build new, powerful, and everlasting strongholds into your life as a True Son or Daughter of God. As an example:*

"The Lord is my rock and my fortress and my deliverer, My God, my rock, in whom I take refuge; My shield and the horn of my salvation, my stronghold." Psalm 18:2

STRONGHOLD EXAMPLES

Below are examples of the 3 ways in which a stronghold can be formed.

Example 1: Emotional Wounding Memory Stronghold

You are 4-years-old in Kindergarten and you wear glasses. The children on the playground make fun of you and call you Four-Eyes. As a little child, this is very hurtful. But as the years pass, you get over it. Or so you think. However, at the time that wounding happened, the enemy started a stronghold on your soul. The enemy took ground on your soul and started building a fortress from which he could then operate. Basically what has happened is that the enemy's forces obtained ground on your soul to harass and torment you by using lies and deceit in order to cause you to come up with the wrong conclusions about yourself (e.g. no one likes you, you are ugly, etc.). Then spirits of rejection, lies, deceit, low self-worth, etc. attach to this stronghold. I picture it as if the enemy has a puppet string attached to that stronghold, and every time similar things happened to you throughout your life, he just tugged on that string a bit to remind you that no one likes you, you are ugly, etc. As you continued to believe those lies, the enemy was then able to add another "brick" to the stronghold, thereby fortifying even more the stronghold from which he was operating.

Now as an adult, someone makes a comment to you. They are just teasing you, but something inside of you flares up in anger! You get offended. Maybe you even stop talking to this person. Maybe you are not able to forgive. Maybe bitterness develops. Why? All because the enemy pulled on that same string and fed you the old lies about your lack of value, etc. - and you believed him!

Know that Jesus wants to set you free!

Example 2: Sin Memory Stronghold

When you were 8 years old, you shoplifted from a store a ring that you just loved. You got away with it and no one ever knew, but you felt so guilty inside. Eventually you got over it and even forgot about it. But as time went on, those feelings of guilt continued to build up because you had stolen something from someone that did not belong to you. You really do not like yourself, but you do not know why. Maybe other similar things like this happened throughout your life. Perhaps you offended people or said mean things to people and never asked them to forgive you. All of these add together to cause self-hatred, self-rejection, and a seared conscience. The enemy, from the beginning when you shoplifted that ring, began a stronghold on your soul. He lied to you and made you feel guilty and ashamed. He told you to lie to cover up your sin. You believed all of his lies. Now as an adult, you have issues, but you are not sure why! You would probably never connect your problems of today with that time you stole the ring as a child.

Thankfully, as you go through the deliverance process, the Holy Spirit will be faithful to remind you of instances such as this, that started a root sin memory stronghold on your soul. As He reveals these things and you repent and ask Him to break the memory stronghold that started way back then, you will begin to feel a release you did not even know you were in need of!

Example 3: Sin Memory Stronghold

There are many cause and effect sequences given in the Bible. With these, it is helpful if we work from the present backwards. Take a minute to assess and see what is manifesting in your life or in your home. Then ask the Lord to reveal if you have violated one of his commands. For example, suppose things are not going well in your home. You have removed anything that would allow ungodly spiritual strongholds. (You will learn more about this later in this book.) You have done all that you know to do. But then the Holy Spirit leads you to this verse: *"He who returns evil for good, evil will not depart from his house."* Proverbs 17:13 You suddenly remember a time when a friend did something very nice for you, but because you were mad at her, you cursed her and did not express any appreciation. Reading this verse convicts you of your sin and at the same time helps you to realize that you are reaping the fruit of what you have sown. (Galatians 6:7) You returned evil for good, and now evil will not depart from your house. This is a type of stronghold that is actually affecting your life at home. First is recognizing it, and then you must repent for it and ask forgiveness of your friend. This is a good example of a sin stronghold, and this is why we must be in the Bible every day, reading and meditating on the things the Lord shows us in His Word.

Example 4: Generational Stronghold

Your grandfather was an alcoholic as was your dad when you were growing up. Eventually your grandfather and your father both stopped drinking and seem fine today. However, you have noticed you have a problem with overspending. You just love to go shopping and you spend a lot of money when you do, racking up credit card debt. It is quite likely that the generational iniquity of alcohol abuse and drunkenness allowed a spirit of addiction to attach to the family line. And in reality, it probably started with generations even before your grandfather's. Nonetheless, this problem with addiction, in whatever form it takes, will continue on through you, your children, and your children's children, if the stronghold is not broken from the family line. Praise God! You have been chosen to do this!

HOW DO I IDENTIFY ALL TYPES OF MEMORY STRONGHOLDS?

The memory strongholds we are going to deal with are **Sin Memory Strongholds** and **Emotional Wounding Memory Strongholds**. There are also **Generational Strongholds**, often referred to as INIQUITIES, which we will learn more on later in this workbook.

In order to identify your own personal memory strongholds, do the following:

- **Get alone with the Lord in a quiet place for at least an hour at a time.** Start off by setting yourself up in the spiritual realm by reading aloud (or quietly) the *Recommended Pre-Session Prayer.*

- **Repent for all unconfessed sin**. Be specific.

- **Black out your mind of all current thoughts** (this sometimes takes a little practice) **and then ask the Lord to bring to mind the memory strongholds of the enemy on your soul**. An area where a "stronghold" exists will come in the form of a memory of something that either you did or something that was done to you. Sometimes what comes to your mind can be seemingly insignificant (like being called "four eyes" as a kindergartener). But no matter how small it may seem, if it comes to mind, write it down.

- **Use the worksheets on the following pages to write down each incident that comes to your mind**. Do not try to analyze these at this point, just write down the memories one by one. If the memory was one where you committed sin, then write it on the *Identifying My Sin Memory Strongholds* sheet. If it is more of an emotional memory of something you experienced in the past, then write it on your *Identifying My Emotional Memory Strongholds* sheet. Once you have made your lists, proceed.

IDENTIFYING MY SIN MEMORY STRONGHOLDS
List Memories of Your Past Sins

IDENTIFYING MY EMOTIONAL WOUNDING MEMORY STRONGHOLDS

List the Memories of Past Emotional Wounds

HOW DO I PREPARE TO GET RID OF ALL TYPES OF MEMORY STRONGHOLDS?

Understand that our weapons are not of the flesh but of the Spirit.
"For though we walk in the flesh, we do not war according to the flesh, for the weapons of our warfare are not of the flesh, but divinely powerful for the destruction of fortresses (strongholds). We are destroying speculations and every lofty thing raised up against the knowledge of God, and we are taking every thought captive to the obedience of Christ..." II Corinthians 10:3-5

Understand that our struggle is not against flesh and blood.
"Our struggle is not against flesh and blood, but against the rulers, against the powers, against the world forces of this darkness, against the spiritual forces of wickedness in the heavenly places." Ephesians 6:12

Once we understand these things, then with the Holy Spirit's help, we will be able to start identifying what the enemy strongholds are. We are looking for the root issues. Whatever memory the Holy Spirit has brought to mind, it is likely a root issue.

Prepare to renounce the lies of the enemy attached to these strongholds. *Identify and write down the lies that you believed about yourself or others at or after the time of the incident.*

Do the Prayer to Break Memory Strongholds.

DEALING WITH MY
SIN MEMORY STRONGHOLDS

Once you have read through the entire book, you will come back to your Sin Strongholds and use the prayer below.

PRAYER TO BREAK SIN STRONGHOLDS

Father, in Jesus name, I ask that You take back the ground that was given to the enemy when I (list the sins one by one). *I repent of having done these things and ask for Your forgiveness. I also ask that You break these strongholds from my soul.*

NOTE:

1. **Renounce** by name the specific sins you committed. (Example: *I renounce fornication. I renounce lies and deceit. I renounce pride.* Etc.)

2. **Announce** what God desires to give you in sin's place. (Example: *By God's grace, I announce that I embrace purity. I announce that I will live in truth. I announce that I will embrace humility.* Etc.) Allow yourself to be led by the Holy Spirit as you come into agreement with God. He tells you His ways in His Holy Word and by His Spirit. Be as specific as He leads you to be. This should be an intimate time with you and your Heavenly Father. **THEN...**

3. **Cleanse and Heal**: At the end of each session, when you have completed the process of breaking the strongholds, ask the Lord to with the blood of Jesus Christ cleanse and heal your soul and every part of your body defiled by the enemy.

4. **Fill** Ask the Lord to give you a fresh filling of His Holy Spirit, so that all places vacated by the enemy will be filled and inhabited by Him.

5. **Command** all demons by name to leave you now and go to Jesus to be dealt with. (Be sure you have read, studied, and understand the section *Demons and the Spiritual Realm* before doing this final step.)s

DEALING WITH MY EMOTIONAL WOUNDING MEMORY STRONGHOLDS

After you have finished the book and made the list of the strongholds from all of the emotional wounding memories the Holy Spirit has brought to your recollection, then go ahead and pray the following prayer. With emotional wounding memories, do each one separately and really spend time making sure it has been thoroughly dealt with. The Holy Spirit will help you.

Father, in Jesus name, I ask that You take back the ground that was given to the enemy when (Fill in the Incident). This incident caused me to feel (Fill in the Emotional Responses you had and the Lies you received from the Enemy at that time). I renounce all of the lies and negative thoughts I bought into as a result of this incident, and I ask that You break every stronghold from my soul.

By an act of my will, I choose to forgive (that person), and I ask that You give me Your GRACE to do so. (See the *Prayer to Grant Forgiveness* to thoroughly deal with necessary forgiveness and to release this person, as the Lord would have you to.)

After doing the above for each incident, then:

1. **Cleanse and Heal**: At the end of each session, when you have completed the process of breaking the strongholds, ask the Lord to with the blood of Jesus Christ cleanse and heal your soul and every part of your body defiled by the enemy.

2. **Fill** Ask the Lord to give you a fresh filling of His Holy Spirit, so that all places vacated by the enemy will be filled and inhabited by Him.

3. **Command** all demons by name to leave you now and go to Jesus to be dealt with. (Be sure you have read, studied, and understand the section *Demons and the Spiritual Realm* before doing this final step.)

WALKING OUT YOUR FREEDOM
AS YOU MOVE FORWARD

Bring every thought into captivity.
Philippians gives us good guidelines for mental hygiene. *"Rejoice in the Lord always; again I will say, rejoice! Let your gentle spirit be known to all men. The Lord is near. Be anxious for nothing, but in everything by prayer and supplication with thanksgiving let your requests be made known to God. And the peace of God, which surpasses all comprehension, will guard your hearts and your minds in Christ Jesus. Finally, brethren, whatever is true, whatever is honorable, whatever is right, whatever is pure, whatever is lovely, whatever is of good repute, if there is any excellence and if anything worthy of praise, dwell on these things. The things you have learned and received and heard and seen in me, practice these things, and the God of peace will be with you."* Philippians 4:4-9

Seek to obey Christ in everything you do.
This requires that we know what Christ asks of us by reading His Word daily. *"'If you love Me, you will keep My commandments.' Jesus answered and said to him, 'If anyone loves Me, he will keep My word; and My Father will love him, and We will come to him and make Our abode with him. He who does not love Me does not keep My words; and the word, which you hear is not Mine, but the Father's, Who sent Me.'"* John 14:15, 23-24

Take confidence in the fact that you are being set free in Christ Jesus.
"If the Son, therefore, shall make you free, you shall be free indeed!" John 8:36

Be careful to no longer give the enemy an "opportunity" to attach to your soul. If you fail at this, ask the Lord to break any stronghold off as soon as you realize you have given him an opportunity (or license).

    "...do not give the devil an opportunity." Ephesians 4:27

(Opportunity = a place, room, area, or location)

WHEN OTHER MEMORIES SURFACE
AS YOU MOVE FORWARD

As you are going about life now and things come to your mind (float up), say the *Breaking Strongholds Prayer* right on the spot.

"Father, in Jesus' name, I ask that You take back the ground that was given to the enemy and break every stronghold from my soul."

In that same moment or even at the end of the day, ask the Lord to apply His blood to your soul to cleanse and heal the areas where the strongholds of that day have been broken off. Once that is done, ask Him to continue revealing other strongholds that need to be broken.

Note: Even if you know you have broken a stronghold, but the incident floats up to your mind again, break it again. And keep breaking it until it no longer comes to your mind. Keep working on this until the goal below defines you.

THREE OF GOD'S GOALS FOR YOU

- *To live completely in the PRESENT.*

- *To no longer be tormented by incidents of the PAST.*

- *To no longer fear the FUTURE.*

TESTIMONIES FROM BREAKING STRONGHOLDS

Victory Over Anxiety (24-Year-Old Woman) *So, I have a really cool testimony. Today I found out that an assignment I submitted two weeks ago didn't actually submit, and because it's past the due date, I can't resubmit it. I've contacted the instructor and told him what happened, and now I'm praying that he'll take my word for it and allow me to submit it without penalty, even though he has no reason to believe that I'm being truthful. The amazing part is that I'm not stressed or anxious about it at all. Worry isn't consuming me about it, as it once would have. Yay for breaking strongholds!*

Woman Who Attended Deliverance For Christians Class (50-Year-Old Woman) *Since I've been attending the Deliverance For Christians' class, I feel like orange or onion peelings are being taken off of me layer by layer. The new me is coming out! It's a wonderful feeling! I am sleeping better too! This scripture comes to mind this morning as to what the Lord is doing in me. II Corinthians 3:18 (NLT) "So all of us who have had that veil removed can see and reflect the glory of the Lord, and the Lord who is the Spirit makes us more and more like him, as we are changed into his glorious image."*

Freedom From Pain of Losing Biological Father Through Divorce (40-Year-Old Woman) *While you and I were praying for my deliverance, we had spoken about my pain from my biological father and the Holy Spirit led us to pray over this. While we were praying I felt like a stem was being pulled out of me, all the way from the root. I felt it being yanked out. All of a sudden, I could breathe more deeply than I ever could before! It felt so strange, but I could actually feel the root coming out! You and I both sensed it was gone and finished. God is so good. Thank you for teaching us about deliverance. It is so important for the Bride of Christ.*

Marriage On The Brink Of Divorce Due To Adultery (50-year-old Couple) *My husband says he feels like a new man and that the Holy Spirit came upon him again this morning when he was praying to God. I think this is amazing! I can't wait to see what*

God has in store for him. Thanks for being there for both of us last night.

<u>Young Man Delivered From The Effects Of Childhood Molestation</u> (24-year-old Man) *I wanted to text you and thank you for everything you have done for me. I love you and have grown so much through your guidance and healing. A year ago from TODAY was when we had our first deliverance. I just want to say that what you do changes lives. God uses you tremendously and may you be blessed abundantly in Him. Have a wonderful day!*

WHAT ABOUT FORGIVENESS?

Scripture is very strong on the fact that it is God's will that we forgive everyone - no matter what he/she has done to us or to our loved one. In fact, there are testimonies that have been given indicating that one could end up in hell if there is unforgiveness in the heart. If you read the below verses with that thought in mind, you may be surprised at how the Bible does seem to indicate that. Why? Because unforgiveness is evidence that you are not walking in the true Spirit of God. We must take forgiveness extremely seriously – because God does.

WHY MUST WE FORGIVE EVERYONE?

Because He has forgiven us.
"Be kind to one another, tenderhearted, forgiving each other, just as God in Christ also has forgiven you." Ephesians 4:32

Because if we do not forgive, it allows a root of bitterness to start that can defile others and us.
"Pursue peace with all men, and the sanctification without which no one will see the Lord. See to it that no one comes short of the grace of God; that no root of bitterness springing up causes trouble, and by it many be defiled..." Hebrews 12:14-15

So that Satan does not have an advantage over us.
"But one whom you forgive anything, I forgive also; for indeed what I have forgiven, if I have forgiven anything, I did it for your sakes in the presence of Christ, so that no advantage would be taken of us by Satan, for we are not ignorant of his schemes." II Corinthians 2:10-11

Judgment will be merciless to the one who has shown no mercy
"Judgment will be merciless to the one who has shown no mercy..." James 2:13

Because if we do not forgive, He will not forgive us!
"For if you forgive others for their transgressions, your heavenly Father will also forgive you. But if you do not forgive others, then

your Father will not forgive your transgressions." <u>Matthew 6:14-15</u>

<u>Because if we do not forgive, He will turn us over to torturers.</u>
"Then summoning him, his lord said to him, 'You wicked slave, I forgave you all that debt because you pleaded with me. 'Should you not also have had mercy on your fellow slave, in the same way that I had mercy on you?' "And his lord, moved with anger, handed him over to the torturers until he should repay all that was owed him. "My heavenly Father will also do the same to you, if each of you does not forgive his brother from your heart." <u>Matthew 18:32-35</u>

<u>Note</u>: *See special testimony of unforgiveness in John Bevere's book: "The Bait of Satan" (pages 123-124).[3]*

---

[3] John Bevere, *The Bait of Satan, 20th Anniversary edition: Living Free from the Deadly Trap of Offense"* (Charisma House, 2014) 123-124

HOW OFTEN MUST I FORGIVE?

Our forgiveness must not end!

"Be on your guard! If your brother sins, rebuke him; and if he repents, forgive him. And if he sins against you seven times a day, and returns to you seven times, saying, 'I repent,' forgive him." Luke 17:3-4

"Then Peter came and said to Him, "Lord, how often shall my brother sin against me and I forgive him? Up to seven times? Jesus said to him, "I do not say to you, up to seven times, but up to seventy times seven." Matthew 18:21-22 (Note: Go on to read the rest of the chapter where Jesus gives a parable about forgiving.)

HOW CAN I FORGIVE?

We can do nothing without Him. It takes **GOD'S GRACE**, which we receive at salvation, to forgive. At salvation, we are given a certain measure of grace and we grow into more grace from there. I like to tell people that God does not give us all the grace He has to give us at once – or our bodies would explode! However, when we hit a situation - like having to forgive someone who has deeply wronged us - *we can ask Him for an extra measure of His Grace to do what we are not able to do ourselves.*

GOD'S GRACE
IS
God operating through you to give you His desire and His power to do His will.

We know that it is always God's will to forgive. Therefore, when we ask Him for His Grace, He will give us both the desire and the power to forgive others. With severe or deeply entrenched offenses, we may have to start with an act of our will by "choosing to forgive" – not because we feel like it, but because we want to obey God.

"And He has said to me, 'My grace is sufficient for you, for power is perfected in weakness.' Most gladly, therefore, I will rather boast about my weaknesses, so that the power of Christ may dwell in me." II Corinthians 12:9

"I can do all things through Him who strengthens me." Philippians 4:13

IF I WAS THE OFFENDER, HOW DO I GO TO SOMEONE TO ASK FOR FORGIVENESS?

Ask the Lord if there is anyone you need to go to in person to ask forgiveness of. If so, here are some recommended steps of action:

Do not say, I'm sorry..." or "I apologize..."

It is not recommended that you say, "I'm sorry" or "I apologize." These words tend to feel to the other person like you are slapping a Band-Aid on his pain. Doing this does not get to the root pain for you - or for the other person.

Instead say: *"(Name), God has convicted me of how wrong I was to (wrong actions/words) to you, and I would like to ask you to forgive me. Will you forgive me?"*

Asking for forgiveness in this manner actually kills pride. It is not the easy way, but it is God's way and He will reward you! Remember: *Godly sorrow leads to repentance.* See II Corinthians 7:10. We need to be repentant and we need to be willing to be humble.

Be sure to receive a "yes" answer from each person.

If you need to add more words to convince the person that you are sincere in your asking for his or her forgiveness, then you may have to do that. However, most of the time, when asking in the above manner, people are more shocked than prideful - and they will usually say they forgive you right away.

- Remember: This is about clearing YOUR conscience for GOD'S sake and your own sake, so that you can eventually achieve the highest levels of Freedom in Christ.

- It is also about activating forgiveness in the other person's heart as well, so that he/she will not suffer punishment or possibly even hell fire for not forgiving you and for harboring bitterness.

53

"For if you forgive others for their transgressions, your heavenly Father will also forgive you. But if you do not forgive others, then your Father will not forgive your transgressions." <u>Matthew 6:14-15</u>

"If you forgive the sins of any, their sins have been forgiven them; if you retain the sins of any, they have been retained." <u>John 20:23</u>

<u>LAST BUT DEFINITELY NOT LEAST</u>

Do not forget to forgive yourself for the things you hold against yourself. Be specific.

TESTIMONIES OF GRANTING FORGIVENESS

Losing Excess Weight After Breaking Strongholds and Granting Forgiveness 50-Year-Old: *I just wanted to tell you how free I feel since you led me in prayer to break off strongholds of painful memories and grant forgiveness by an act of my will to those who had wronged me. I know I need a lot more prayer, but I have been able to lose weight and before it had been almost impossible for me to stick to a diet. I feel great and I truly believe that something was lifted off of me that night when we prayed! Thank you so much!*

Granting Forgiveness to Ex In-Laws
30-Year-Old Woman: *I am officially a freedom junky! Praise report! God is so good! He set me free from the pain of my ex-husband's parents today. He freed me from their resentment towards me and He is also having me write a letter to them, asking for their forgiveness! Praise God! I literally feel like my eyes got brighter and my heart got softer! My attitude right now is: Bring it on Jesus! Let's do this!*

ON THE LIGHTER SIDE

Regarding the passage from Matthew 6:12, "*Forgive us our trespasses as we forgive those who trespass against us,*" one little boy prayed, "*And forgive us our trash baskets, as we forgive those who put trash in our baskets.*"

MY FORGIVENESS LIST

People I Have Had A Hard Time Forgiving
OR
People who have hurt me and I am having a hard time getting over the hurt.

Put a √ next to the ones the Holy Spirit tells you that you need to go to in person to ask forgiveness of.
Try to do this as soon as possible.

After making your list, go to the next page and do the *Prayer to Grant Forgiveness* over each person who has offended you - one by one.

NOTE: Most of the time, we were at least 5% wrong in any given situation where offense was taken. Sometimes the Lord will have you go to someone to ask forgiveness for your 5%, so that person can then forgive you and not be in danger of the eternal judgment of God. See Matthew 6:14-15. As well, most of the time when we take this initiative, the other person will ask your forgiveness as well. When we understand that God does not forgive a person who has unforgiveness in his heart, it will make it easier to want to help that person forgive – as God has forgiven us.

LIST

PRAYER TO GRANT FORGIVENESS

Father, in Jesus name, I ask that You take back the ground that was given to the enemy when (Name of Person) (List Specific Incidents). *I ask that You break every stronghold from my soul. And as an act of my will, I choose to forgive* (Name of Person) *and I ask that You give me Your Grace to do so, from the bottom of my heart.*

REMINDER
GOD'S GRACE is God working through us to give us His desire and His power to do His will.

Remember: It is always God's will to forgive.

I renounce unforgiveness. I renounce bitterness, and I ask that You remove every root of bitterness. If anyone has been defiled by my bitterness, I ask that You show me who that is and what I need to do.

I ask that You bind the enemy from (Name of Person); *take off all the veils of the enemy; and open his eyes, ears, heart, and soul to the truth of God. I also ask that You bring someone to him who can lead him to salvation.*

I release (Name of Person) *now to You, Lord, for You to work in his heart, soul, and life, as You will.*

At this point, picture letting go of this person as you would a helium balloon and allow him to float up to God for God to work with him as He knows is necessary to bring him to repentance.

After praying for each person the Holy Spirit has brought to your mind to forgive, finish this session with the following final steps:

1. **Cleanse and Heal** Ask the Lord to cleanse and heal your soul and every part of your body defiled by the enemy with the blood of Jesus Christ.

2. **Fill** Ask the Lord to give you a fresh filling of His Holy Spirit, so that all places vacated by the enemy will be filled and inhabited by Him.

3. **Command** all demons by name to leave you now and go to Jesus to be dealt with. (Be sure you have read, studied, and understand the section *Demons and the Spiritual Realm* before doing this final step.) Potential demons that might be attached would be: spirits of unforgiveness, bitterness, resentment, pride, self-hatred, etc. – as the Holy Spirit brings to mind.

Note: Always be in tune to what the Holy Spirit is putting on your mind and let Him guide you. These prayers are formulated to cover the necessary spiritual warfare "bases." He will lead you into healing, give you special words of knowledge or wisdom, etc. if you allow Him to - by giving Him your time with this.

FORGIVENESS: WALKING IT OUT

STEPS OF ACTION WHEN I HAVE BEEN OFFENDED

1. **Give yourself until sundown or AT MAX 24 hours** to ruminate over the situation, but NO LONGER than this.

   a. You may discuss your situation with ONE other person ONLY, IF NECESSARY to help with processing. However, this person must be someone who will help you towards forgiveness (as opposed to taking up your offense with you). This discussion too must cease at the 24-hour mark, so let that person know ahead of time what your plans of action are and that his "job" is very temporary (24 hours). (We have to be especially careful of sharing with someone else, because often that person will then have a bad attitude towards the person who hurt you…and he could end up with a forgiveness issue of his own that he then has to deal with.)

"Be angry, and yet do not sin; do not let the sun go down on your anger, and do not give the devil an <u>opportunity</u>."
<u>Ephesians 4:26-27</u>

<u>Opportunity</u> = *a place, room, area, or location*. (I believe that is what is implied from what we now understand about strongholds is the addition of – *from which to operate*.)

2. At the 24-Hour point:

   a. Do the *Prayer to Grant Forgiveness*.
   <u>Remember</u>: GRACE is the secret ingredient!

   b. **Release (like a helium balloon) that person to God**. That person is now in His hands and you must trust that He will take care of it. He will chasten, as He knows is necessary. Sometimes He will chasten even more than we would! If we follow these steps of action, by the time the Lord chastens that person, you will have forgiven them so thoroughly, that YOU may be the one the Lord uses to pick them up and encourage them! And that is the gift of mercy and grace in action!

    c. **<u>Cease thinking about it</u>!** Completely cease! This cannot be stressed enough. Understand that you choose what to think about, so choose to no longer think about the offense. Cut it loose and let it go to God for Him to deal with it, as He wills.

3.   <u>Result</u>: In a few days, if you have done the above, you will forget what that person even did to you, and restoration of the relationship will happen – as is God's desire. (Remember: It is only the enemy who loves division.)

WHAT IS THE DIFFERENCE BETWEEN SIN, TRANSGRESSION, & INIQUITY?

There is a Progression of
SIN to TRANSGRESSION to INIQUITY to DEATH

*" "Then, when **desire** has **conceived**, it gives **birth** to **sin**; and **sin**, when it is **full-grown**, brings forth **death**."."* James 1:15

WHAT IS SIN?

- Sin is something that is contrary to the nature of God.
- It is that which deserves punishment.
- It is that which is morally wrong.
- It is that which is an offense.
- It is that which causes one to stray from God.
- Relative to transgression and iniquity, we will say that sin is "skin deep." Sin is anything that comes short of the glory of God. Sin, if left unchecked and not repented for, will lead to a downward spiral and eventually become transgression.
- What should we do about sin? REPENT! *"If we confess our sins, He is faithful & righteous to forgive us our sins and to cleanse us from all unrighteousness."* I John 1:9
- There are many other verses about sin. To learn more, search for "sin" on *Bible Gateway* or other such resource.

WHAT IS TRANSGRESSION?

- Repeated sin becomes a form of rebellion and is categorized as transgression.
- Transgression is a willful deviation from, and therefore rebellion against, the path of Godly living.
- It oversteps the limits.
- It is the practicing of sin in that it becomes part of our lifestyle.
- Strong's Dictionary (H6588) says *transgression is a revolt or rebellion.*
- Transgression is also characterized as presumptuous sin, which is knowing the right thing to do and still choosing to

do the wrong thing. *"Also keep back Your servant from presumptuous sins; Let them not rule over me; Then I will be blameless, And I shall be acquitted of great transgression."* Psalm 19:13

- Sin left unchecked becomes transgression and this continues to spiral downward towards iniquity.

WHAT IS INIQUITY?

- If one still does not repent and continues on, the wrongs then becomes iniquity (or bondage).
- Iniquity signifies not merely that which is wrong, but the tendency to do wrong.
- It is second nature sin, which drives us to repeatedly, continually commit sin.
- It is a perversion of the truth, which leads to error.
- It is a perversion of intents, which affects our wills.
- It is the bent condition of what we are. (Sin and Transgression are things we DO. Iniquity becomes part of who we ARE.)
- Iniquity causes an entrenchment in and a perversion of the flesh.
- It revolves more around underlying attitudes (e.g. idolatry, covetousness, unrighteousness, racism, gluttony, **wickedness, lawlessness, etc.).**
- It involves our attitude, so it cannot just be covered over with blood. It must be **taken away and replaced.** In Psalm 51:10 David prayed for a new heart and a right Spirit.
- It is not superficial. It is under the skin; It is deeply imbedded like bruises. Isaiah 53:5 *"...He was crushed for our iniquities..."*
- It gives us a crooked arrow to start with - as opposed to sin, which is like having a chain around your ankle, which constantly hinders you. Sin trips us up; it causes us to slip, to err, and to miss the mark. Iniquity is deeply rooted.
- Iniquity is a premeditated choice that will continue, if it is not repented for. (A Biblical example is David's sin with Bathsheba. It was premeditated. He plotted evil first in his heart, then in his actions, and finally in his words. We

know that his propensity for sexual iniquity was then passed on to at least one of his sons named Amnon who raped and then abandoned his half-sister Tamar. 2 Samuel 13

<u>INIQUITIES ARE OFTEN (IF NOT ALWAYS) GENERATIONAL</u>

"The LORD, the LORD God, compassionate and gracious, slow to anger, and abounding in lovingkindness and truth; who keeps lovingkindness for thousands, who forgives iniquity, transgression and sin; yet He will by no means leave the guilty unpunished, visiting the iniquity of fathers on the children and on the grandchildren to the third and fourth generations." Exodus 34:6-7

Generational iniquity is the iniquity of the forefathers that continues on through the generations because it is "taught" (by word and/or action) by fathers to their children. The Bible tells us in I Peter 1:18 that our *"futile way of life was inherited from our forefathers."* (Forefather = ancestor.)

Strong's Dictionary (H5771): 1) Perversity, depravity, iniquity, guilt, or punishment of iniquity. 1a iniquity, 1b) guilt of iniquity, guilt (as great), guilt (of condition) 1c) consequence of or punishment for iniquity. [4]

Note from Author: As an update to this material, I have come to believe that the practice of iniquity CHANGES our DNA – and that iniquitous DNA is passed to us. We did not cause it, we did not ask for it, but we have a weakness for that particular iniquity and if we are not careful, we will come into agreement with that iniquity through the sin in our own lives – and make it our own!

"For I, the LORD your God, am a jealous God, visiting the iniquity of the fathers on the children, and on the third and the fourth generations of those who hate Me…" Deuteronomy 5:9

---

[4] https://biblehub.com/parallel/psalms/51-2.htm

WHAT IS THE OUTCOME OF CONTINUING INIQUITY?

God will chasten you and you will not prosper. *"With reproofs You chasten a man for iniquity; You consume as a moth what is precious to him..."* Psalm 39:11

You will die (both spiritually and physically) and go to hell. *"But when a righteous man turns away from his righteousness, commits iniquity and does according to all the abominations that a wicked man does, will he live? All his righteous deeds, which he has done, will not be remembered for his treachery, which he has committed, and his sin, which he has committed; for them he will die."* Ezekiel 18:24 *(continue reading to verse 30)*

"And I prayed unto Jehovah my God, and made confession, and said, Oh, Lord, the great and dreadful God, who keeps covenant and lovingkindness with them that love him and keep his commandments, we have sinned, and have dealt perversely, and have done wickedly, and have rebelled, even turning aside from thy precepts and from Thine ordinances..." Daniel 9:4-5

You will become a hypocrite. *"Do not drag me away with the wicked and with those who work iniquity, who speak peace with their neighbors, while evil is in their hearts."* Psalm 28:3

You will not fear God and therefore you will not have wisdom - because the fear of God is the beginning of wisdom. (See Proverbs 9:10.) *"Transgression speaks to the ungodly within his heart; there is no fear of God before his eyes. For it flatters him in his own eyes concerning the discovery of his iniquity and the hatred of it."* Psalm 36:1-2

You will be ensnared in wickedness and held with cords of sin. *"His own iniquities will capture the wicked, and he will be held with the cords of his sin."* Proverbs 5:22 (The Lord showed me during a deliverance session years ago that there are literal "cords of iniquity" that are attached to us at birth, even in the womb.)

RESULTS OF THE PROGRESSION OF SIN
ACCORDING TO THE BIBLE

YOU WILL: (See Romans 1:18-25)

- Suppress the truth in unrighteousness.
- Know God but not honor Him as God or give thanks to Him.
- Become futile in your speculations.
- Have your foolish hearts darkened.
- Profess to be wise but become fools.
- Exchange the glory of the incorruptible God for an image in the form of corruptible man and of birds and four-footed animals and crawling creatures.
- Exchange the truth of God for a lie.
- Worship and serve the creature rather than the Creator.

GOD WILL: (See Romans 1:26-32)

- Give you over to degrading passions (including homosexuality).
- Give you the due penalty of your error.
- Give you over to a depraved mind, to do those things which are not proper, being filled with all unrighteousness, wickedness, greed, evil; full of envy, murder, strife, deceit, malice; they are gossips, slanderers, haters of God, insolent, arrogant, boastful, inventors of evil, disobedient to parents, without understanding, untrustworthy, unloving, unmerciful; and although they know the ordinance of God, that those who practice such things are worthy of death, they not only do the same, but also give hearty approval to those who practice them.

SOME WAYS TO DEAL WITH INIQUITY

Know that Jesus died for our iniquities. *"But He was pierced through for our transgressions, He was crushed for our iniquities; the chastening of our well-being fell upon Him; and by His scourging, we are healed."* Isaiah 53:5

Confess and repent of iniquity committed - not only by you but also by your forefathers. *"If they confess their iniquity and the iniquity of their forefathers, in their unfaithfulness which they committed against Me, and also in their acting with hostility against Me...then I will remember My covenant with Jacob, and I will remember also My covenant with Isaac, and My covenant with Abraham as well, and I will remember the land."* Leviticus 26:40, 42

If you sow to iniquity, you will harvest trouble. *"According to what I have seen, those who plow iniquity and those who sow trouble harvest it."* Job 4:8

Purpose not to commit iniquity. *"I was also blameless toward Him, and I kept myself from iniquity."* 2 Samuel 22:24

Learn to be humble of heart. *"...or if their uncircumcised heart becomes humbled so that they then make amends for their iniquity, then I will remember My covenant with Jacob, and I will remember also My covenant with Isaac, and My covenant with Abraham as well, and I will remember the land."* Leviticus 26:41 & 42

If you commit iniquity, repent! *"Now David's heart troubled him after he had numbered the people. So David said to the Lord, "I have sinned greatly in what I have done. But now, O LORD, please take away the iniquity of Your servant, for I have acted very foolishly."* 2 Samuel 24:10

Do not hide your iniquity. *"I acknowledged my sin to You, and my iniquity I did not hide; I said, "I will confess my transgressions to the LORD"; and You forgave the guilt of my sin. Selah."* Psalm 32:5

Do not go along with men who practice evil deeds. *"Do not incline my heart to any evil thing, to practice deeds of wickedness with men who do iniquity; and do not let me eat of their delicacies."* Psalm 141:4

We are to rebuke our children (even as adults) if they are involved in iniquity. *"For I have told him that I am about to judge his house forever for the iniquity which he knew, because his sons brought a curse on themselves and he did not rebuke them."* I Samuel 3:13 (Note: Rebukes to adult children should be done ONE time. We are not to continually rebuke them because this becomes abusive and we begin to sound like a "clanging cymbal." Rebuke one time, and then stand back and pray.)

Show lovingkindness and truth. *"By lovingkindness and truth, iniquity is atoned for…"* Proverbs 16:6

Show mercy to the poor. *"Break away from sins by doing righteousness and from iniquity by showing mercy to the poor…"* Daniel 4:27

Do not have idols but rather love God and keep His commandments! *"You shall not make for yourself an idol, or any likeness of what is in heaven above or on the earth beneath or in the water under the earth. You shall not worship them or serve them; for I, the LORD your God, am a jealous God, visiting the iniquity of the fathers on the children, on the third and the fourth generations of those who hate Me, 6 but showing lovingkindness to thousands, to those who love Me and keep My commandments."* Exodus 20:4-5

Repent of iniquities, and God will give pardon *"The LORD is slow to anger and abundant in loving-kindness, forgiving iniquity and transgression; but He will by no means clear the guilty, visiting the iniquity of the fathers on the children to the third and the fourth generations. Pardon, I pray, the iniquity of this people according to the greatness of Your lovingkindness, just as You also have forgiven this people, from Egypt even until now. So*

the LORD said, "I have pardoned them according to your word..."
Numbers 14:18-20

TESTIMONY FROM SOMEONE WHO DEALT WITH GENERATIONAL INIQUITIES

Victory Over Fear of Man and Lust 25-Year-Old Man: *I have something exciting to share! I have always had a hard time looking people in the eyes. Girls are the hardest. Two days ago I repented of fear of man from my forefathers. The next day, I was with friends & there were a couple of girls hanging out with us. I started looking people in the eyes. I couldn't stop making eye contact and communicating with the girls very openly. I wasn't scared. I wasn't nervous. It was awesome! I would say that it changed 80% overnight. This may seem insignificant, but it makes me so excited! Everywhere I go I am able to look people in the eyes. I am not sure why, but I feel like that is huge! Since going through everything in Level 1, so much has changed! I used to take medication for anxiety. Now I don't take anything! I sleep so much better! Purity is something that I have gone to great measures to protect for years, but now it is literally impossible to not think and act without complete purity. The freedom in all this is beyond words! I am so grateful both to you and most importantly to Jesus! People see me laughing, or dancing and it might not make sense, but sometimes I just can't hold in the amount of freedom that I feel.*

SCIENCE AGREES

Our DNA
- *Contains coding*
- *Mutates*
- *Genes are the part of the DNA that encodes information.*

Monarch Butterflies The Monarch butterfly appears to pass its knowledge and memories via genetics on to its offspring (from generation to generation). From this, scientists were able to then use this knowledge to use in Project Monarch mind-controlled victims, believing that they pass down their programming to their children. [5] (More in *Deliverance For Christians Level 3*.)

Study on Mice (Decembers2013) *"A provocative study of mice reports that certain fears can be inherited through the generations. The authors suggest that a similar phenomenon could influence anxiety and addiction in humans."* [6]

Animal Studies (December 2013 BBC): A few statements from the article: *"Animal studies suggest that behavior can be affected by events in previous generations which have been passed on through a form of genetic memory, experiments showed that a traumatic event could affect the DNA in sperm and alter the brains and behavior of subsequent generations, changes in brain structure were also found, and it is thought that a signal from the brain was sent to the sperm to alter DNA."* [7]

---

[5] https://news.uchicago.edu/article/2014/10/06/genetic-secrets-monarch-butterfly-revealed

[6] https://news.uchicago.edu/article/2014/10/06/genetic-secrets-monarch-butterfly-revealed

[7] http://www.bbc.com/news/health-25156510

DEALING WITH GENERATIONAL INIQUITIES

The descendants of Israel separated themselves from all
foreigners, and stood and confessed their sins
and the iniquities of their fathers.
Nehemiah 9:2

On the following page starts a list of potential generational
iniquities. The list is long, but it is important that we confess and
repent of each one on behalf of ourselves and our forefathers.

Recommended Prayer
<u>Note</u>: *Go to the Throne Room before God the Father to pray.*

"Father God, I choose to stand in the gap for my forefathers to
repent and ask Your forgiveness on behalf of them and myself for:
*[and then read off all the iniquities under "**ABUSE**"].*

I also choose to stand in the gap to repent and ask Your
forgiveness on behalf of my forefathers and myself for: [and then
*read off all the iniquities under "**ADDICTIONS**"].*

I also choose to stand in the gap to repent and ask Your
forgiveness on behalf of my forefathers and myself for anything
that we did that caused: [and then read off all the possibly sin-
*related tendencies/illnesses under "**DISEASE/ILLNESS**"].*

Continue on doing the same thing for each category.

FINISHING PRAYER
"I thank you Father God, for Your forgiveness. I ask that you sever
every generational cord of iniquity from me and from all future
generations. I ask that You wash me inside and out with the blood
of Jesus Christ, completely removing the defilement of the enemy
from me. I ask that You remove all iniquitous DNA within me and
replace it with the cleansed and unblemished DNA that You
intended me to have. I ask that You create in me a clean heart.
Give me a heart of flesh and take away any part of my heart that is
stone. And I ask that You renew a right spirit within me. Amen!

GENERATIONAL INIQUITIES (TENDENCIES) IN MY OWN FAMILY

Pray through all of the following and repent on behalf of your forefathers.

ABUSE *Can stem from putting Self in place of God.*

Controlling of others
Emotionally abusive to self or others
Mentally abusive to self or others
Physically abusive to self or others
Sexually abusive to self or others
Spiritually abusive to self or others
Substance abuse (drugs, alcohol, prescription meds, etc.)
Torture to self or others
Verbal abusive to self or others
Other_____

ADDICTIONS *Addiction is a sinful response to life's trials.*

Alcohol addiction
Collection addiction
Computer games addiction
Computer media forms addiction
Drug addiction (prescription or illegal)
Food addiction (Gluttony)
Gambling addiction (in any form)
Pornography addiction
Reading addiction (rare but possible)
Sex addiction (in any form)
Shopping addiction (on line or in person)
Sugar addiction
Tobacco addiction
TV addiction
Work addiction
Other_____

DISEASE/ILLNESS IN YOUR FAMILY LINE
NOTE: Much illness & disease has spiritual roots. Ask the Lord to reveal any root reasons for the following and then repent and ask Him to break off all roots from you.
Accident-prone

DISEASE/ILLNESS *(Continued)*

Alzheimer's
Anorexia/Bulimia
Arthritis
Asthma
Autism
Back problems
Bacterial infections
Blindness
Bone and joint problems
Cancer
Chronic pain
Compulsive behavior (Obsessive-Compulsive)
Congestion in Lungs
Cysts
Depression
Diabetes
Early death (before age 70)
Emphysema
Epilepsy/Seizures
Fatigue
Female problems
Forgetfulness
Heart disease
Hypochondria
Insanity
Insomnia
Loss of limb
Memory dysfunction
Mental blocks
Mental illness: Bipolar Disorder, Schizophrenia, etc.
Mental torment
Migraines
Mind-racing
Multiple Sclerosis
Obesity
Paranoia
Physical abnormalities
Premature death
Scoliosis

DISEASE/ILLNESS *(Continued)*
Senility
Trichotillomania (Pulling out of hair anywhere on body)
Other_____

FEARS *Fear is the absence of faith, trust, & surrender to God.*
Fear of abandonment
Fear of accidents
Fear of being hurt
Fear of being wrong
Fear of certain animals, insects, etc.
Fear of death
Fear of failure
Fear of fear
Fear of illness or disease
Fear of man / People-pleasing
Fear of success
Other_____

FINANCIAL
Bankruptcy
Cheating
Co-signing
Covetousness
Debt
Delinquency
Fraud
Greed/Stinginess
Irresponsible spending
Job failure
Lack
Poverty
Robbery/Stealing
Robbing God (in tithes and offerings)
Slothfulness/Loving Sleep
Tax evasion
Other_____

IDOLATRY *Anything that comes before God in your life.*
Academics (Knowledge)
Celebrities/Famous People
Collectors' Items
Electronics (games, Facebook, etc.)

IDOLATRY *(Continued)*
False gods/religions/religious practices
Fetishes
Friends
Hobbies
Ministry
Music
Possessions (Wealth)
Power (Prestige)
Sports
Your children
Your job
Your spouse
Other_____

OCCULT *All practices involving intentional Satanic input.*
Acupuncture
Animal Spiritism
Astral projection
Astrology
Aura reading
Automatic writing
Black Magic
Conjuring demons
Crystal balls
Curses or spells
Demon worship
Demonic laughing
Demonic sex (Incubus, Succubus)
Dispatching demons
Divination
ESP
Evil eye/Third Eye/Eye of Horus
Familiar spirits
Fascination with evil
Fortune-telling
Handwriting analysis
Hexing
Horoscopes
Hypnosis
Incantations
Invisible Friends
Kinesiology
Levitation
Medium

OCCULT *(Continued)*

Mental telepathy
Mutilation of self or others
Necromancy
New Age practices
Non-Christian exorcism
Occult books
Occult games
Occult movies
Occult music
Ouija board
Palm-reading
Past life readings
Pendulum readings
Psychic healing
Psychic readings
Rebellion
Reincarnation
Ritual abuse
Ritualism
Santeria
Satanism
Séances
Sorcery
Spells
Spirit guides
Superstition
Tarot Cards
Tealeaf reading
Torture
Trance
Transcendental Meditation
Vampirism
Voodoo
Water-witching (Douser)
Werewolf
White Magic
Wiccan/Witchcraft (Warlock/Witch)
Yoga
Other_____

RELIGION

Antichrist following
Atheist
Catholic
Christian Carnality/Liberalism

RELIGION *(Continued)*

Denominationalism
Does not believe in gifts of the Holy
Spirit
Eastern Religion
Excessive rules
Freemasonry
Hypocrisy
Judgmental/Critical
Martial arts
Mormon
Muslim
Other false
religions_____
Overemphasis on works (not grace)
Perfectionism
Rejection of God
Religious Spirit (Law without love.
Legalistic.)
Scientology
Spiritual pride
Traditionalism
Unhealthy fear of God
Other_____

SELF-CENTERED INIQUITIES

Conceit
Egotism
Pride (overt and hidden)
Self-accusation
Self-centeredness
Self-condemnation
Self-deception
Self-hatred
Self-importance
Self-pity
Self-punishment
Self-rejection
Self-sufficiency
Self-will
Selfishness
Suicide
Suicide fantasies
Vanity
Victim mentality
Other_____

SEXUAL	OTHER
Abortion	Abandonment
Adopting children out	Accusation
Adultery	Anger/Rage
Barrenness	Anguish/Sad/Sorrow/Misery/Gloomy
Bestiality	Arrogance
Blocked intimacy, Frigidity	Betrayal/disloyalty
Cheating/unfaithfulness	Bitterness
Cross-dressing	Blaspheming
Cyber Sexual Activity	Broken vows
Enticing/Seducing	Cheating
Fantasy Lust	Complaining/murmuring
Flashing	Condemnation
Flirtatious	Confusion
Fornication	Contempt/Hatred
Homosexuality (Gay/Lesbian)	Contentious (argue/bicker)
Impotence	Critical
Incest	Cruel
Infidelity	Crying/Weeping
Lewdness	Daydreamer
Lust	Deception
Masturbation	Defeat Defiance
Miscarriage	Defilement
Molestation	Denial
Nudity (inappropriate)	Deportation
Orgies	Desertion
Pedophilia	Despair/Despondency
Perversion	Destruction
Polyamory	Discouragement
Polygamy	Disgrace
Pornography	Dishonesty
Pregnancy out of wedlock	Disobedience
Prostitution	Division
Rape	Domineering/controlling
Sadomasochism, etc.	Double-mindedness
Sexual inadequacy	Doubt
Sexual perversion	Driving zeal
Transgender	Embarrassment
Voyeurism (Watching others in their	Enabling
private sexual activities, nudity, etc.	Entrapped
Includes watching this on TV or other	Envy/Jealousy
forms of media as well as in real life.)	Extreme competition
Other_____	Failure
	False responsibility
	Fantasy
	Feuding

Fret/Worry
Frustration
Gossip
Guilt
Hallucinations
Harassment
Haughtiness
Heartbreak
Heaviness
Helplessness/Hopelessness
Hoarding
Hostile
Hysterical
Inadequacy
Independence
Inferiority/Not being good enough
Injustice
Insecurity
Insubordination
Intimidating
Irresponsible
Isolation
Jail/Juvenile Delinquent
Lacks self-control
Loneliness
Loss
Lying
Manipulation
Military (Branch and rank)
_____

Mistrust
Murder
Negative Thought Processing
Neglect
Nervousness
Organized crime
Over-sensitivity
Passive
Passive aggression
Possessiveness
Prejudice
Pressure to succeed
Procrastination
Profanity
Rationalizes/Blames others

Rejection of others
Resentment
Resistance
Restlessness
Revenge
Ridicule/Mocking
Rivalry
Sarcasm
Scorn
Secrecy
Separation
Shame
Skeptical
Slanderer
Strife
Striving
Stubbornness
Suspicion
Temper tantrums
Timidity
Torment
Trauma
Treachery (pretending to be close to someone to get something you want)
Treason
Trickery
Uncertainty
Uncleanness
Undermining
Unfaithfulness
Unforgiveness
Untrustworthiness
Violence
Withdrawal
Other_____

LIST ANY OTHERS BELOW OR ON BACK OF THIS PAGE:

On the next page is a **Family Tree** where you can list the names and iniquities of people in your family line. This is often helpful in being able to see what is affecting you and your children, in order to take steps to repent and renounce the iniquitous tendencies and set up personal boundaries to help alleviate falling into sinful patterns where the family line is weak.

Some suggested **Family History Codes** (abbreviations) are given below, so that you can get as much as you want on this chart.

FAMILY HISTORY CODES

Here are some suggested codes to shorten the amount of writing on the family history form.

A	Anger problems
AD	Adultery (with whom)
BU	Buddhist
C	Christian
CA	Catholic
CNW	Calls self a Christian but not walking with Lord (Note: May not be truly saved.)
D	Divorce
DI	Died (add year if known, or your age at time of their death, if you remember)
FM	Freemason (add level)
IN	Incest (with whom)
L	Lust problems
M	Married (add number of years and happy, unhappy, had to, etc.)
MO	Molestation (to whom)
NC	Not a Christian
O	Occult Involvement
RA	Rape (whom)
RM	Remarried (Name of second spouse)
SRA	Satanic Ritual Abuse
W	Witchcraft involvement

ADD YOUR OWN CODES AS NEEDED

Family Tree

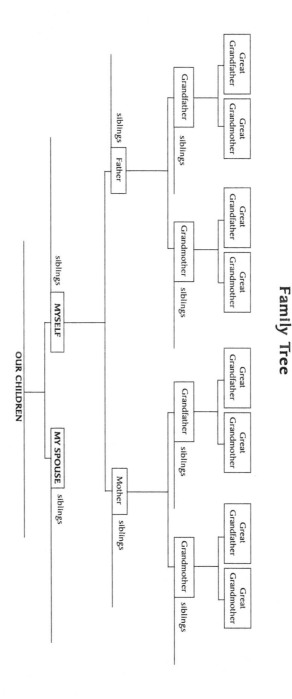

MY FAMILY'S GENERATIONAL INIQUITIES

This is a chart to list the major iniquities running through your family line on both sides. (Use more paper as needed.)

Father's Name:_____

Iniquity	Number of Relatives	Names (Optional)

Mother's Name:_____

Iniquity	Number of Relatives	Names (Optional)

CURSES CAN COME UPON US

By worshipping false gods and/or coming into agreement with false religions *"You shall have no other gods before Me. You shall not make for yourself an idol, or any likeness of what is in heaven above or on the earth beneath or in the water under the earth. You shall not worship them or serve them; for I, the LORD your God, am a jealous God, visiting the iniquity of the fathers on the children, on the third and the fourth generations of those who hate Me..."* Exodus 20:3-6

By denying that God exists *"If we deny Him, He also will deny us."* 2 Timothy 2:12

By blaspheming (including denying the power of) **the Holy Spirit** (unforgiveable sin). *"Then a demon-possessed man who was blind and mute was brought to Jesus, and He healed him, so that the mute man spoke and saw. All the crowds were amazed, and were saying, "This man cannot be the Son of David, can he?" But when the Pharisees heard this, they said, "This man casts out demons only by Beelzebub the ruler of the demons." And knowing their thoughts Jesus said to them, "Any kingdom divided against itself is laid waste; and any city or house divided against itself will not stand. "If Satan casts out Satan, he is divided against himself; how then will his kingdom stand? "If I by Beelzebub cast out demons, by whom do your sons cast them out? For this reason they will be your judges. "But if I cast out demons by the Spirit of God, then the kingdom of God has come upon you." Or how can anyone enter the strong man's house and carry off his property, unless he first binds the strong man? And then he will plunder his house. He who is not with Me is against Me; and he who does not gather with Me scatters. Therefore I say to you, any sin and blasphemy shall be forgiven people, but blasphemy against the Spirit shall not be forgiven. Whoever speaks a word against the Son of Man, it shall be forgiven him; but whoever speaks against the Holy Spirit, it shall not be forgiven him, either in this age or in the age to come."* Matthew 12:22-32

By violating sexual laws Leviticus 18

By dishonoring parents *"Children, obey your parents in the Lord, for this is right. Honor your father and mother (which is the first commandment with a promise), so that it may be well with you, and that you may live long on the earth."* Ephesians 6:1

Through consequences of our own sins (disobeying God). Principle is in Deuteronomy 28:15-28

By broken vows to God *"When you make a vow to God, do not delay to fulfill it. He has no pleasure in fools; fulfill your vow. It is better not to make a vow than to make one and not fulfill it. Do not let your mouth lead you into sin. And do not protest to the temple messenger, "My vow was a mistake." Why should God be angry at what you say and destroy the work of your hands? Much dreaming and many words are meaningless. Therefore, fear God."* Ecclesiastes 5:4-7

"I shall pay You my vows, which my lips uttered, and my mouth spoke when I was in distress." Psalm 66:13-14

By those who practice witchcraft and sorcery. Isaiah 47

By the generational sins and iniquities of the forefathers
Exodus 20:4-5 and Exodus 34:7 (This is one reason why repenting for and asking the Lord to sever these from us is so important.)

By having iniquity in our lives *"With reproofs You chasten a man for iniquity; You consume as a moth what is precious to him; Surely every man is a mere breath. Selah."* Psalm 39:11

By word curses spoken over us by self or others (often by a "well-meaning" loved one or an enemy) *"Death and life are in the power of the tongue. And those who love it will eat its fruit."* Proverbs 18:21 (See section *What are Word Curses.)*

List Other Ways Curses Can Come Upon You, As Revealed To You By God

_____

_____

_____

_____

_____

_____

_____

_____

_____

_____

_____

_____

I THOUGHT WE WERE NO LONGER SUBJECT TO CURSES

Some will try to refute the concept of a curse on a Christian using the following verses. Be prepared to answer these arguments by understanding the below.

A curse without a cause cannot alight. Proverbs 26:2
This is true, but it requires that the enemy have no strongholds on you. Almost no one lives in this state of freedom unless he/she has been through extensive deliverance and set free.

Christ has redeemed us from the curse of the law.
Yes, He has redeemed us from the curse of the LAW - but NOT the curse of God as a consequence for disobedience.

> ***Obedience brings blessing. Disobedience brings cursing.***
> (See Deuteronomy 30:15-20.)

We will reap what we sow. *"Do not be deceived, God is not mocked; for whatever a man sows, this he will also reap. For the one who sows to his own flesh will from the flesh reap corruption, but the one who sows to the Spirit will from the Spirit reap eternal life."* Galatians 6:7-8

That is Old Testament: *"When Pilate saw that he was accomplishing nothing, but rather that a riot was starting, he took water and washed his hands in front of the crowd, saying, "I am innocent of this Man's blood; see to that yourselves. And all the people said, <u>"His blood shall be on us and on our children!"</u>* (And it has been!) <u>Matthew 25:24-25</u>

<u>Note</u>: Those of Jewish decent must ask the Lord to break this curse spoken over them by their forefathers.

WHAT ARE WORD CURSES?
The Power of the Tongue

"But I tell you that every careless word that people speak, they shall give an accounting for it in the Day of Judgment. For by your words you will be justified, and by your words you will be condemned." Matthew 12:36-37

"DEATH AND LIFE ARE IN THE POWER OF THE TONGUE."
Proverbs 18:21

The Spoken Word is VERY Powerful

Example: God SPOKE the world into existence! (Genesis)

Proverbs 10
- *The mouth of the righteous is a fountain of life.* (11)
- *On the lips of the discerning, wisdom is found (13), but with the mouth of the foolish, ruin is at hand.* (14)
- *He who conceals hatred has lying lips.* (18)
- *He who spreads slander is a fool.* (18)
- *When there are many words, transgression is unavoidable.* (19) (Note: If you are going to sit and talk to people for a long time, it is best to focus all talk around the Word of God.)
- *The tongue of the righteous is as choice silver.* (20)
- *The lips of the righteous feed many.* (21)
- *The mouth of the righteous flows with wisdom (but the perverted tongue will be cut out).* (31)
- *The lips of the righteous bring forth what is acceptable (but the mouth of the wicked what is perverted).* (32)

We do not mean to be "abusive," but we are, and verbal abuse is relative. For example: *"You are no help!"* in one family can be just as damaging as *"You are stupid!"* in another family. Many people have been raised in homes where they were spoken to very negatively or even abusively by parents.

What causes parents to speak abusively?

- The need to control, which usually comes out of fear and anxiety, often stemming from their own past hurt and pain.
- Their parents spoke abusively to them.
- Insecurity about their roles as parents.
- Allowing a battling of the wills rather than using a rod to discipline children, as the Bible tells us to. (When parents do not spank, "reasoning" and the battle of the wills ensues. This eventually leads to verbal abuse in most cases, especially as the child gets older.)
- Note On Parenting: You have about the first 12-13 years of your child's life to TRAIN him in the ways of the Lord, as the Bible instructs us to. After that age, you will begin to reap what you have sown – and you will see how you have done in your parenting role.

Many people have been raised in homes where they were spoken to very negatively or even abusively by siblings.

What causes siblings to speak abusively?

- Older siblings are given too much responsibility over younger siblings.
- One sibling may want another sibling to do well and/or not get in trouble with the parents, so "motivational" words, though well intended, can sometimes become abusive.
- One or more siblings may have feelings of low self-esteem, which can manifest as jealousy and/or sibling rivalry, etc., which can eventually also turn to abuse.

You do not have to be speaking directly to a person to generate a word curse against him/her. Our words go into the atmosphere and begin a motion.

Example: *"Furthermore, in your bedchamber do not curse a king, and in your sleeping rooms do not curse a rich man, for a bird of the heavens will carry the sound and the winged creature will make the matter known."* Ecclesiastes 10:20

What are the ways we speak death to or over each other?

- When we gossip
- When we are anxious
- When we are angry or frustrated
- When we try to seduce
- When we try to control
- When we try to manipulate
- When we are fearful
- When we flatter

What is the difference between speaking life – and flattery?

- Flattery is the act of giving excessive compliments, generally for the purpose of getting on the good side of the person being flattered.
- Flattery is insincere and/or excessive praise.
- The Bible says, *"A flattering mouth works ruin."* Proverbs 26:28
- See also: Psalm 12:2-4, Proverbs 26:24-28, Proverbs 29:5, Romans 16:17-19.
- To combat flattery, instead speak words of love coupled with gratitude for the internal character qualities and integrity that we see in the person. Character qualities are things such as diligence, servanthood, giving, loving, going the extra mile, etc.
  - Example: *"Thank you for so diligently doing your chores today."*
  - See the following page for a list of some Godly character qualities to praise in others.

SOME GODLY CHARACTER QUALITIES
TO PRAISE IN OTHERS

Accountability	Discretion	Joyfulness	Respect
Alertness	Endurance	Justice Kindness	Responsibility
Amends	Enthusiasm	Knowledge	Reverence
Attentiveness	Fairness	Leadership	Righteousness
Authenticity	(Equity)	Love	Security
Availability	Faith	Loyalty	Self-Control
Benevolence	Faithfulness	Meekness	Sensitivity
Boldness	Fear of the	Narrowness	Servanthood
Bonding	Lord	Nurture	Sincerity
Boundaries	Firmness	Obedience	Stewardship
Breadth	Flexibility	Optimism	Strength
Brotherliness	Forgiveness	Orderliness	Surrender
Candor	Friendship	Originality	Teachability
Caution	Generosity	Passionate	Thankfulness
Cheerful	Gentleness	Patience	Thoroughness
Chivalry	Gladness	Peaceful	Thoughtfulness
Commitment	Goal-	Perseverance	Thriftiness
Compassion	oriented	Persuasiveness	Tolerance
Confidence	Goodness	Poise	Transparency
Consistency	Gratefulness	Prayerful	Truthfulness
Contentment	Greatness	Prosperity	Trusting
Courage	Holiness	Prudence	Trustworthy
Creativity	Honesty	Punctuality	Understanding
Decisiveness	Honor	Pure speech	Unstoppable
Deference	Hope	Purity	Virtuous
Dependability	Hospitality	Purposeful	Visionary
Determination	Humility	Reasonableness	Vulnerability
Diligence	Indignation	Renewal	Wisdom
Discernment	Initiative	Resourcefulness	Worshipful
Discipline	Integrity	Restoration	

HOW CAN WE SPEAK LIFE TO EACH OTHER?

- Stop to think before we speak.

- Say things (even bad things) in a positive way. See following examples:
  o Rather than, *"Can't you, please* (with frustration in your voice) *take out the trash?"* say *"Would you be able to take the trash out for me today?"* (With a smile)
  o Rather than, *"What's wrong with you?"* say, *"Are you okay?"*

- In Ezekiel 37, Ezekiel had a prophetic vision of his speaking life over the dry bones, and with the right words, he was able to bring them to life again. So, God wants to bring all of us out of our "graves." He wants to bring us to life! He wants to bring us to unity and One Accord with one another and with Him.

ADDITIONAL IMPORTANT NOTES ON CURSES

- **Words We Sing**: The Lord recently reminded me that we must also be aware of the words we sing! If you have sung along to ungodly songs in the past, ask the Holy Spirit to bring to mind the things you have sung, so that you can ask Him to cancel those words of death over yourself or others. (Example: "*I'll never love again.*") We also need to be careful of words we sing even in Christian songs. As times get darker, the enemy gets more sinister and more deceptive. Be sure you know what words you are singing and to whom you are singing them. Often the music can be so beautiful or catchy that we get caught up in that and do not listen to the words we are singing over ourselves.

- **Words We Speak in Places Like Recovery Groups**: When recovering addicts of all sorts get up to speak in certain kinds of meetings, they are often first required to say, for example, *"Hello, my name is Bill and I am an alcoholic."* This must be cancelled as a perpetual word curse over the person. It might also be wise to encourage the person to seek help from other sources such as local churches, deliverance ministries, etc. that are about breaking word curses rather than perpetuating them.

- **Jewish**: If you are of Jewish descent, you may be under a curse from God because of the disobedience of your forefathers and you are under the blood curse spoken by Pilate in the New Testament. These need to be broken off of you after you have received Christ as your Savior. (See *Prayer to Renounce The Curse Of Pilate On The Jews.*)

  o **The Curses For Disobedience In The Old Testament** (passed through the generations via generational iniquities). See Leviticus 26:14-46 and Deuteronomy 28:15-68.

o **<u>The Curse Spoken Over The Jews By Pilate</u>** *When Pilate saw that he was accomplishing nothing, but rather that a riot was starting, he took water and washed his hands in front of the crowd, saying, "I am innocent of this Man's blood; see to that yourselves." And all the people said, "His blood shall be on us and on our children!"* <u>Matthew 27:24-25</u>

PRAYERS TO ERADICATE POSSIBLE CURSES
OVER MY LIFE

I want to preface this by saying, when you are ready to say the prayers to ask the Lord to break off the curses over you and your life, PLEASE GO TO THE THRONE ROOM AND SPEAK DIRECTLY FACE-TO-FACE WITH OUR FATHER GOD.

You will find this so much more powerful and life changing when you do this, because it builds an intimacy and faith in God than what I call "yelling your requests up to Heaven."

If it were your earthly Father, you would not go into the house and yell up the stairs, "Hey Dad, I'm sorry I got angry today and called you a bad name" and expect that everything will be as good as if you went upstairs and sat down before your father and talked to him face-to-face about whatever you wanted to talk to him about – good or correctional. Let's do the same with our Heavenly Father. It will be to YOUR benefit. Begin to make it your habit to go to the throne room as often as you can when you want to speak to God Our Father.

Let's proceed.

Start here by making a list of the specific instances representing each way a curse has been generated over your life. Once you have made your list, then go ahead and pray the specific prayer to break that particular curse over your life. Feel free to say the given prayer and add in, as you feel led by the Holy Spirit.

If unsaved people are involved, it is recommended that you add in the following prayer: Father, in Jesus' name, I ask that You bind the enemy from (Name of Person); *take off all the veils of the enemy; and open his eyes, ears, heart, and soul to the truth of God. I also ask that You bring someone to him who can lead him to salvation. And I release him now to You, for You to work in his life, as You will.*

Blaspheming the Holy Spirit: Speaking against the gifts and power of the Holy Spirit. See Matthew 12:22-32.

> Prayer: *Father God, in Jesus' name, I repent for speaking or even just disbelieving that the Holy Spirit's gifts and power are for every generation throughout all of time until You come again. I ask that You break any curse from me for my disbelief and that You would fully activate within me – all of the gifts and fruits of Your Holy Spirit.*

Broken Vows to God See Ecclesiastes 5:5 and Psalm 50:14-15.

> Prayer: *Father God, in Jesus' name, I repent for breaking this vow that I made to You. I understand that vows are very important to You and I ask that You give me Your grace to fulfill the vow I made to You from this time forward.*

Dishonoring Parents See Ephesians 6:1-3 & Deuteronomy 27:16.

> Prayer: *Father God, in Jesus' name, I repent for dishonoring my parents. I understand that honoring my father and mother is a command from You and that regardless of whether I agree with them or not, I must choose to honor them. Give me Your grace to do so.*

Disobedience See Deuteronomy 28:15.

> Prayer: *Father God, in Jesus' name, I repent for* (List Acts of Disobedience). *I ask for Your forgiveness, Lord. I ask for Your grace to obey You from this time forward. If I do disobey You, I purpose in my heart to repent quickly and not allow sin to crouch at my doorway.*

Evil Words Spoken or Sung Over Me See Proverbs 18:21, Make a list of what was said/sung and by whom, including yourself.

> Prayer: *Father God, in Jesus' name, I repent for and ask that You would cancel all word curses I have sung over myself or my loved ones. Specifically, I ask that You cancel:* (List the Word Curses.)

I am Jewish.

The Jews are under a curse from God that needs to be broken from them, once they receive Christ as Savior.

- **The Curses For Disobedience In The Old Testament** (passed through the generations via generational iniquities). See Leviticus 26:14-46 and Deuteronomy 28:15-68. (If you are of Jewish descent, turn to these passages and begin to confess and repent of the disobedience of your forefathers and then name and ask God to cancel each curse (listed in these passages) from you and your future generations.

- **The Curse Spoken Over The Jews By Pilate** Matthew 27:24-25

Prayer To Renounce The Curse Of Pilate On The Jews

Father, in Jesus' name, I choose to stand in the gap for my forefathers confessing and repenting of their sins and their iniquities. Specifically, I repent of the wicked desire and willingness of my forefathers to prefer Barabbas (the sinner) over Jesus (the Savior); I repent of their desire to see Jesus crucified on the cross of Calvary; I repent of their wanting their way so much that they were willing to say, "His blood shall be on us and on our children!" Father, forgive me for all of these things.

I announce that it is that blood of Jesus Christ of Nazareth that was shed on that cross. That blood atones for all of my sin and sets me free from the penalty of death. It is that blood that was shed that marks Him as my Lord and Savior. I serve my Father God by following His Son Jesus Christ in all of His ways. And I have been given the Holy Spirit of God to help me to walk in righteousness and to be transformed from darkness into light, as I work out my own salvation with fear and trembling. I will live eternally in Heaven with my Savior forever and ever. To Him who loves us and released us from our sins by His blood, and who has made us to be a kingdom, priests to His God and Father—to Him be the glory and the dominion forever and ever. Amen. Revelation 1:5-6

I was in a recovery organization (and I spoke word curses over myself such as, *"Hello, my name is___and I am an alcoholic."*)

> Prayer: ***Father God, in Jesus' name, I ask that You cancel the perpetual word curse I have been speaking over myself in my recovery meetings by continuing to identify myself as (fill in this blank). By Your grace I ask for forgiveness and I ask that I be identified first and foremost as a Child of the Most High God, who is King over all.***

Violating Laws of Man and God (including tithing - see Malachi 3:8-11) Use the *Worksheet On Biblical Curses And Natural Consequences Of Sin* on the next page for ongoing help in this area.

> Prayer: ***Father God, in Jesus' name, I recognize that You have set certain laws in motion for we, Your people, to navigate by. These laws are for our great good. I confess and repent for violating the laws You have brought to my attention. Specifically, I repent for:*** *(List your violations and consequences that you have noticed.)* ***By an act of my will and by Your grace, I purpose in my heart to be obedient to the Laws of both Man and of God.***

Other

FURTHER STUDY ON BIBLICAL CURSES AND NATURAL CONSEQUENCES OF SIN

There are many cause and effect statements in the Bible. As you study the Word, keep a list here. If you are having a certain problem in your life or home, you can work backwards from the manifestation. Example: If there is a lot of evil going on in your house, look up scriptures on "evil." You may find, as below, that you or someone in your home "returned evil for good" to someone, and that needs to be confessed, repented for, and made right with that other person, so that God can then lift that consequence for sin from your home. Proverbs is an especially good place to find cause-effect statements of the Lord.

REFERENCE	SIN	CURSE
Proverbs 17:5	Rejoicing at calamity	You will be punished
Proverbs 17:13	Returning evil for good	Evil will not depart from your house
Malachi 3:8-9	Not giving tithes or offerings.	You are cursed with a curse for robbing God.

PRAYER TO BREAK CURSES

Breaking curses is not a once and done thing. Periodically, it is good to do this because there can be new people who are angry or upset with you, who are speaking word curses over you. Be self-aware of unusual things that are happening to you without seeming cause. These things could be happening as a result of a curse and/or spell being generated towards you. Remember to include cancelling and breaking off words sung over you from ungodly songs, words spoken over you at certain types of self-help meetings, curses by Pilate over the Jews, and/or curses by God for sin.

Father, in Jesus name, I ask that You break every generational curse spoken over the family line by my forefathers. Specifically, I ask that You cancel every ungodly vow, promise, agreement, or assignment of the enemy over my family. I specifically renounce all false religions and false idols – namely Freemasonry, Buddhism, witchcraft, etc. (Note: If you or your family have been involved with certain religions, deeper breaking of specific vows made will need to be done as well. See *Deliverance For Christians Level 3* for more information on this.)

I announce that my family and I will serve the one and only true and living God of the universe. I announce life over my family. I announce righteousness, blessing, and Godliness over my family. (Continue on as Holy Spirit brings to mind.)

Father, in Jesus' name, I also ask that You cancel the curse that was spoken over me by _____ when he/she said_____

_____

_____

I ask that You cancel every word curse I have spoken over myself. Specifically that I_____

_____

_____

I ask that instead you would bless me (with opposite of what was spoken). By an act of my will I choose to forgive_____ and myself, and I ask that You give me your grace to do so.

I also ask that You cancel all of the word curses that I, myself, have spoken over others! Specifically, when I said_____
_____
to/about _____. I ask that You cancel what I said and give him/her a blessing instead.

And, Father, I ask that You cleanse my body inside and out with the blood of Jesus, removing all defilement of the enemy from me.

WHAT ARE SPELLS?

- Spells are cast by those who believe they can use the power of Satan to control and/or manipulate others.

- When our forefathers have been involved with occult activities (e.g., rituals, superstitions, witchcraft, witchdoctors, etc.), the spells they generated can and will affect future generations. Many times these spells were generated with the "intent to conquer evil" but one cannot fight evil with evil. And that deceptive practice can sometimes, for the moment, appear to help, but eventually it will lead to death, as is always Satan's ultimate goal. With people who use occult practices to try to fight "evil," the result often is that a spirit of death comes over the family line (manifesting as troubled relationships, divorce, trouble with finances, literal early death, etc.).

- In modern times, children have learned (via the internet, movies, books, etc.) that they can cast spells.

- Spells and curses are easily found on the Internet.
  - *Cast a spell to bring back your lover*
  - *Cast a spell to get more money*
  - *Cast a spell to fix serious problems*
  - *The Couple-Buster Curse*
  - *The Breakup Spell*
  - *The Evil-Eye Spell*
  - *The Get-Even Spell*

- At the *California Astrology Association* website any spells or other paraphernalia that you purchase for that purpose comes with the following guarantee: ***"At the California Astrology Association, we understand that you might be skeptical about the power of spell casting, metaphysics, and astrology. But we're not. We are so sure that our products and services will work for you; we offer an unconditional ONE-YEAR money back guarantee. So, you've got nothing to lose!"*** [8]

Note: *They boast at having had this guarantee since 1970, which shows us that casting spells on others is not new.*

Note: If you go to this website, be sure to put yourself in isolation first.

- Therefore, if strange things are happening to you (hair falling out, accidents, unusual contention between loved ones, etc.), consider that someone might be casting a spell on you.

- Certain types of people who are involved in occult practices can often discern the powerful Christians in their community that are a threat to them - and they will render ritual spells against the Christians and/or even seek to gain entrance to the church or ministry to affect it as an "insider."

[8] http://www.calastrology.com/

PRAYER TO BREAK SPELLS

Father, in Jesus' name, I ask that You cancel every spell and every curse that is being sent my way by those whose motives are intentionally sinister. I ask that You also return these spells and curses to the sender with increasing intensity, until they cease this practice. Bring confusion to those they conspire with, who conjure spells and curses, so that they would be unable to continue functioning in this manner. Bind the enemy from each and every one of them, open their eyes to the truth of God, and bring someone to each of them who can lead them to salvation through Jesus Christ alone.

Cover my family, everything we own, and me with the blood of Jesus Christ of Nazareth, and I claim, in Jesus' name, that as the Word of God says – No weapon formed against us will prosper.

Note 1: Evil spells are becoming more and more prevalent towards true Believers in Jesus Christ. Keep this in mind, especially in times when strange things are happening in your home and life. Unusual bouts of sickness are one key indicator we often see. Pray the above prayer to break the spell. If it is an evil spell or curse being sent your way, you will notice a difference almost immediately.

Note 2: If you are feeling particularly oppressed by the words, curses, and/or spells of others, you might consider going to Psalm 35 and read it as a prayer to the Lord, just as David did – and claim the victory that is ours as Children of the Most High God.

DEMONS AND THE SPIRITUAL REALM

Part of The Great Commission:
"These signs will accompany those who have believed: in My name they will cast out demons..." Mark 16:17

In Level 1, we are only giving some very basic ground-level information on the topic of demons and how they can affect our lives. We will go more in depth with this topic in Levels 2 and 3.

Some Possible Manifestations of the Presence of Demons Nearby

- Fear
- Nightmares
- Contention
- Disunity/division
- Confusion
- Sudden cold
- Smell (sometimes like a dead rat or sulfur)
- See something unusual in person's eyes (e.g., spirit of lust, spirit of anger, etc.)
- Nausea
- Sounds without cause (Poltergeists are low-level demons, but they are noisy, and they use noise to try to instill fear.)
- Hair stands up on body *"Then a spirit passed by my face; the hair of my flesh bristled up."* Job 4:15
- Headache
- Feeling of not being alone or someone/something near you
- Just know (discernment)
  - Note: In the spiritual realm, there is no "logical reasoning." One just knows. Thus, sometimes when you "just know" something, it is because it is being spiritually perceived.

NAMES OF DEMONS

Because it would be impossible to know the name of every demon, we name them based on what they do. Almost all types of demons specialize in one function. For example, Spirits of Lust cause lust. Spirits of Fear cause fear. Etc. They likely have other names as well, but unless they tell you what that name is, you do not need to know what it is in order to deal with them. We simply call them by their function.

SOME EVIL SPIRITS MENTIONED IN THE BIBLE

Numbers 5:14	Spirit of Jealousy
Judges 9:23	Evil Spirit (that caused problems)
I Kings 22:21	Enticing/Persuading Spirit
I Kings 22:22-23	Lying/Deceiving Spirit
II Kings 19:7	Spirit of Rumors
Proverbs 16:18	Spirit of Pride, Arrogance Haughtiness
Isaiah 19:14	Spirit of Dizziness, Confusion, Foolishness, Perverseness, Giddiness and/or Distortion
Isaiah 61:3	Spirit of Heaviness, Fainting, Despair, Weakness, Grief
Jeremiah 51:1	Spirit of Destroyer
Hosea 4:12	Spirit of Harlotry (Prostitution, Lewdness, Whoredom, Fornication, Idolatry)
Zechariah 13:2	Unclean Spirit or Spirit of Uncleanness/Impurity*
Mark 9:25	Deaf and Mute/Dumb Spirit (Spirit that will not allow someone to speak or hear)
Luke 13:11	Spirit of Infirmity Disability, Affliction
Romans 8:15	Spirit of Slavery, Bondage
Romans 11:8	Spirit of Stupor, Slumber, Drowsiness, Deep Sleep (Eyes do not See; ears do not hear.)
Acts 16:16	Spirit of Divination, Prediction

	Fortunetelling, Python
I Timothy 4:12	Spirit of Seduction
2 Timothy 1:7	Spirit of Timidity/Fear, Cowardice
I John 4:3	Spirit of the Antichrist
I John 4:6	Spirit of Error, Deception, Lies

* A few teach that unclean spirits are not the same as demons. I personally believe that they are demons but that they manifest as unclean – just as other demons manifest as fear, lust, anxiety, etc. I base this on the following verses:

*"In the synagogue there was a man possessed by the **spirit** of an **unclean demon**, and he cried out with a loud voice."* Luke 4:33

*"For He had commanded the **unclean spirit** to come out of the man. For it had seized him many times; and he was bound with chains and shackles and kept under guard, and yet he would break his bonds and be driven by **the demon** into the desert."* Luke 8:29

*"While he was still approaching, **the demon** (as above) slammed him to the ground and threw him into a convulsion. But Jesus rebuked the **unclean spirit** and healed the boy and gave him back to his father."* Luke 9:42

Note: *In Deliverance For Christians Level 2, you will learn more about the differences between demons and other satanic forces including the angles that followed Satan from Heaven.*

STEPS TO DEMONIZATION

Anyone can be demonized. The extent depends on how much the individual has allowed the demon to have control. We also need to understand that while Satan is behind all demonization, it is rare that he, himself, is the culprit, since he is neither omnipresent nor omniscient. He has an army of forces that work for him and under his authority. Most demons that we deal with at a personal level are actually in the lowest ranks of the Satanic realm. We are not to fear them, but we are to be aware of them and get rid of them. Infiltration of the enemy into our lives is not to be tolerated!

STEP 1: OPPRESSION

Demons oppress Christians to try to get us to give in to whatever it is they want us to do to get us off of God's path for us. *"Hear then the parable of the sower. When anyone hears the word of the kingdom and does not understand it, the evil one comes and snatches away what has been sown in his heart. This is the one on whom seed was sown beside the road."* Matthew 13:18-19

- We can overcome this kind of demon by exercising our own will. God will not, and Satan cannot, decide for us. Our will is completely our own.

- We can and should rebuke demons from oppressing us. Use the simple authoritative statement: *"In Jesus' name, I command you, demon of fear, to get away from me now and go to Jesus to be dealt with. You have no authority over me. I am a child of The Most High God. Be gone!"*

STEP 2: OBSESSION

If we give in to oppression, that can turn into obsession. For example, the temptation to have sex outside of marriage when not overcome by our wills…can then turn into obsession (often recognized as addiction and/or idolatry).

- It is possible to overcome this level by our wills, but it is more difficult to do so, and it often requires us to "bounce along the bottom" a few times before we have enough determination to stop and turn from our sinful ways.

- Demons can enter our bodies at this point because they have license to. Your sin is a stronghold of the enemy that he can, therefore, attach to.

STEP 3: POSSESSION

At the point where we give in to obsession, we step into the danger zone of the demonic moving in and taking up abode within our bodies. We are still responsible for this because we gave in to him at Steps 1 and 2, but we will no longer be able to overcome the demonic without help, deliverance, and following intentional steps of putting Biblical truths into action in our daily lives.

WHEN CASTING OUT DEMONS

Grow in Your Authority in Jesus Christ: In order to effectively cast out demons, you must seek to grow in your authority. Jesus gave you the authority at salvation, but the demonic realm may not immediately recognize your authority. Let us make a note here, too, that a non-Christian has not been given authority by Jesus to cast out demons – as in the example below.

- *"And the evil spirit answered and said to them, 'I recognize Jesus, and I know Paul, but who are you?'" And the man in whom was the evil spirit, leaped on them, subdued all of them, and overpowered them, so that they fled out of that house naked and wounded."* Acts 19:15 (These men were probably not Christians, which is why they were hurt. Nonetheless, even as Christians, we are wise to build up our authority in Christ FIRST.)
- Remember: God gave Jesus His authority. Jesus gave authority to us when He left this earth. (See below verses and *Appendix: Commands of The Great Commission*.)
  - *"Behold, I have given you authority to tread on serpents and scorpions, and over all the power of the enemy, and nothing will injure you."* Luke 10:19
  - *"And He went up on the mountain and summoned those whom He Himself wanted, and they came to Him. And He appointed twelve, so that they would be with Him and that He could send them out to preach, and to have authority to cast out the demons. And He appointed the twelve..."* Mark 3:13-16
  - It is important NOT to take personal pride in our authority. *"Nevertheless, do not rejoice in this, that the spirits are subject to you, but rejoice that your names are recorded in heaven."* Luke 10: 20
- How does one grow in authority?
  - By growing in knowledge and wisdom of the Word of God.
  - By living righteously and above reproach.
  - By practicing our spiritual gifts by faith.

Make sure that you are clean from ongoing sin: Repent of your own sins and ask the Lord to fill you with His Holy Spirit and give you wisdom, truth, discernment, understanding, and any other tools you will need to deal with the demonic.

Educate yourself from reliable sources about the demonic realm: Use *Deliverance For Christians Levels 1, 2, and 3* along with other recommended books and materials. Use discernment as to whether what you are studying is truth or not. Sometimes the only way to know if something will work is by trying what is suggested. Sometimes something that works for one minister does not work for another. You will want to see how God leads you to be used.

Always ask the Lord to bind and cut off all Satanic powers from the highest to the lowest levels, from being able to assist the demons you are dealing with.

Always deal with strongholds first: Even if someone is manifesting, try to have him or her repent of any sin that may be tied in, break the stronghold, confess generational iniquity, and/or renounce the spirit that is manifesting. (Note: Somehow, the demon got license, so it is your job to help figure out how.)

- Note: In our experience, if strongholds are dealt with first, demons will rarely manifest, but rather they will leave on their own when commanded to, because they understand that they no longer have license to remain. In fact, oftentimes they will even leave before they are commanded to because they do not like being told to go to Jesus to be dealt with. When you use this as part of your practice in dealing with the demonic, that message will spread in the spiritual realm – not to mess around with you because of where you will send them.

Always tell the demons where they are to go whether they visibly manifest or not.

- We know that *"where two or three are gathered"* in the name of Jesus, He is in the midst. (Matthew 18:20) Therefore, announce to the spiritual realm BEFORE you start commanding the demons to release – that when they are commanded to leave, they must go to Jesus to be dealt with.

If Demons Manifest:

- You take charge.
- Do not show fear. (Fake it until you make it.)
- Do not yell. Demons do not have a hearing problem and heightened voices usually reveal the expression of fear. (Note: Yelling deliverance ministers scare a lot of Christians away from wanting anything to do with deliverance, so there is a dual reason for this not being okay!)
- Ideally, someone should be praying quietly in the Spirit. (If possible, have that person stand behind the person you are working with and lay hands on him/her while praying.)
  - Command the demons: *"Demon of* (name*), come out, in the name of Jesus Christ, and go to Jesus to be dealt with."*
    - Speak in a matter-of-fact tone but with authority.
    - Remember: It is EXTREMELY important to tell the demons to go to Jesus, because otherwise you are at risk for their leaving the person and going into the nearest, weakest person – which might be a child!

- **Troubleshooting**
  - If the demon or demons do not come out:
    - Press in more by insisting they exit at the command of Jesus through you, etc.
    - Have others in the room pray silently. Do not allow people standing around to be shouting at the demons trying to get them out. This just brings confusion. One person takes charge; the others pray and get revelation.
    - Sometimes someone else in the room may carry more authority in a particular area than you. So

be discerning about that possibility and be prepared to hand "the reins" over to that person, if that seems like the best course of action.

- The enemy could still have ground in the person's soul, and you will then need to stop the session and deal with strongholds, generational iniquities, and/or other issues that have allowed the enemy to have license to this person. (Sometimes, if you ask the demon, it will tell you what ground it has.)
- Call for warring angels to help.
- Using a cross in front of the face can be helpful. They hate the cross.
- Sometimes just laying a Bible on someone helps.
- Anointing oil on the forehead can be helpful. (Demons seem to hate the smell of anointing oil.)
- Use God's Word to rebuke the demonic as Jesus did in Matthew 5.

o If the demon throws the person around:
- Command it to stop manifesting. "I forbid you to manifest in any physical way."
- If that does not stop them, clear objects out of the way, so that person does not hurt himself. Again, if demons have "legal rights," then we are often limited on what we can do until those legal rights are dealt with. The demons know this.
  - It is best if you can get the person down on the ground and then hold legs and other parts of the body.
  - No matter what, take control.
- At any time, you can speak directly to the person and tell him to come to the front. *"Bill, come to the front!"* That will bring the person front and push the demon back. This is especially helpful and necessary if it appears

that there is going to be violence, and someone is in danger of getting hurt - including the person himself.

- o Limit the demons speaking to you. Do not get sucked into engaging in conversation with the demons. Only get the info you need, and then move on.

- Finishing a session: Always finish a session by asking the Lord to bind any other demons that may still remain. Ask Him to cleanse and heal the person inside and out with the blood of Jesus. And then pray a fresh filling of him/her with the Holy Spirit in all places vacated by the enemy.
  - o Note: Binding the demons only lasts for so long, so get back to working with the individual as soon as possible. Resuming within a week or less is the ideal.

- Give instruction: The person needs instruction on how to walk out his freedom. This is where knowledge of the Word of God and its practical application in daily living is extremely important for every deliverance minister.

- Pray for one another on your team. The satanic realm will always attempt to counterattack. We must stay vigilant against these counterattacks and know what our weapons of warfare are. (See *Deliverance For Christians Level 2.*)

CAN CHRISTIANS HAVE DEMONS?

(Also, see *Christians Can Be Demonized* in Appendix section called *Deliverance Verses*.)

COME LET US REASON TOGETHER

ARGUMENT 1: *Light and dark cannot coexist.*

- This is false. Light and darkness MUST coexist because we still live in a fallen world. We Christians, as light, live in the midst of darkness on a daily basis. We constantly coexist side-by-side with the darkness.
- We also know that Satan is, at times, called by God to visit the throne room, as he did in Job 1:6. This is another instance of light (God) and dark (Satan) being "together."
- Therefore, we can conclude: This is a faulty argument.

ARGUMENT 2: *Jesus cast out demons before His followers had the Holy Spirit. Now that we have the Holy Spirit in us, we cannot have demons in us.*

- It is correct that Jesus did cast demons out of the Jewish people before they had the Holy Spirit. However, they were under the Law that was available to them for their time. Therefore, they were covered by God and were considered by Him to be His people.
- In Matthew 12:43-45, we see that *"...when the unclean spirit goes out of a man, it passes through waterless places seeking rest and does not find it. Then it says, 'I will return to my house from which I came' and when it comes, it finds it unoccupied, swept, and put in order. Then it goes and takes along with it seven other spirits more wicked than itself, and they go in and live there; and the last state of that man becomes worse than the first."*
  - We can conclude from this that it is, therefore, generally unwise to cast demons out of unbelievers.
  - Christians, on the other hand, who are "swept clean" and have the Holy Spirit to "fill" the vacant places," can therefore not have the demons come back seven

times worse as in the case with those who have nothing with which to fill the unoccupied spaces.

- As Jesus was leaving this earth, He gave what is commonly referred to as *The Great Commission* to all who would be living on in His name and for His glory, seeking to continue doing on earth what He did while He was here. (See *Appendix: Commands of The Great Commission.*) Specifically, Mark 16:15-18 says, *"And He said to them, 'Go into all the world and preach the gospel to every creature. He who believes and is baptized will be saved; but he who does not believe will be condemned. And these signs will follow those who believe: In My name they will cast out demons; they will speak with new tongues; they will take up serpents; and if they drink anything deadly, it will by no means hurt them; they will lay hands on the sick, and they will recover.'"*

o Therefore, we can conclude:
  - Since we are generally not to cast demons out of the unsaved AND
  - We are commanded by Jesus at His ascension to cast out demons in His name, THEN
  - The primary group of people from whom we would be casting out demons would be Christians.

ON CHRISTIANS CANNOT HAVE DEMONS

If a demon or demons are known to manifest in a Christian's life, other Christians will often say, "Well then that person was not really saved." This is possible. However, because of this, we cannot say, "Christians cannot have demons" together with "Once we are saved, we are always saved." Either we have to face the fact that Christians can have demons...or we have to face the fact that many people who call themselves Christians are not saved. We cannot have it both ways. To give the answer in response to demons manifesting in the church of, "They were never saved..." is not sufficient. We either have to face the fact, once again, that Christians can have demons, or we have to recognize that many in our churches are not saved – or BOTH. Either way, we have a lot of work to do!

Note: As you process this information, some of the following studies done on-line may help you as you increase your knowledge and understanding of this sometimes-controversial topic within the Body of Christ.

TESTIMONIES OF THOSE SET FREE
FROM DEMONIC INFILTRATION

Victory Over Tension & Anger 30-Year-Old Christian Woman: *So far, what I have noticed since the prayers on Thursday is that, I am more relaxed. I have a sense of peace within me. For as long as I can remember I have always had "tense" shoulders. I feel as if they have loosened up and I have a lot less pressure. Last week I had a lot of anger in me; it is now gone. I don't know if I have told you this before but after every session we have had, I have felt drained and exhausted, so when I get home, I sleep and when I wake up, I feel more refreshed than ever. Thank you for your time and for teaching me so much.*

Physical Benefits Of Freedom After 5-Hour Deliverance Session 40-Year-Old Christian Widow: *I can breathe deeply through both nostrils. My ears are unplugged. The pain behind my eyes is gone and has not returned. My sinus cavities are empty. This type of non-pain continues all the way down to my feet. My feet are steady. I can stand still without wobbling. I went to my home study group and sat where people could see me without cringing. It is a MIRACLE!*

Deliverance From Python Spirit 23-Year-Old Christian: *I don't know if I ever told you, but I have been in a complete spiritual awakening ever since my deliverance. I see God with new eyes. I can't explain it. He has fixed my eyes on the Gospel of Christ like never before. (I had been a religious zealot. My deliverance was all rooted in religion. It was wrapped around me like a cord.) I am singing a new song and it feels so good. God used my deliverance very instrumentally to prepare me to love my husband unconditionally. Thanks again for the very important role you have played in setting me free and helping me fall more in love with Christ.* (More on *Python Spirit* in *Level 2*.)

CLEANSING YOUR HOME OF ENEMY STRONGHOLDS

I want to preface this teaching by making a very clear statement that we sometimes do not think about in today's world: **GOD DOES NOT WINK AT SIN!**

Why is this statement so important? Because we, as Children of God, have let our standards slip when we are behind closed doors. Many think nothing of watching movies or television with demonic horror, fornication, homosexuality, foul-language, violence, drunkenness, etc. Know that you will be held accountable for the things you allow your eyes to see and your ears to hear, and even more so when we allow our children or teens to be within earshot/eyeshot of these things and/or even allow them to watch along with us. Question: *Would you allow your neighbors to come in and fornicate on your living room floor while you and your children watched? If not, then why do you allow that (and other such things) on your living room television?*

We turn now to cleansing our homes of strongholds for a number of reasons. First, we want our homes to be pure, sanctified, holy places of rest for us from the world. Cleansing is an important first step in the process of getting the enemy out of our lives. Often we as Children of God do not realize that we have actually given the enemy a right to be in our homes. We can "invite" the enemy in and/or or give the enemy "license" to be there by the things we have allowed in our homes.

There are a few ways that you can tell if the enemy has infiltrated your home.

- If anyone has **nightmares**

- If anyone has **fear**, especially of the dark (even children)
  We tend to think it is "normal" for children to fear the dark, but it is not. If they fear the dark, it is because there are demonic forces there that the child is sensing. Demons of fear actually project fear and children are often more sensitive than adults in picking up on that. Take your child

114

seriously if he is telling you that he sees or senses things or that he fears "something"

- If there is **contention** amongst family members or people that live in the home

In today's world, there are many things (including children's toys, games, movies, etc.) that will attract the enemy to your home and allow him license to be there. Our recommendation is that you get rid of these things by burning what you can and breaking what you cannot. <u>Acts 19:18-19</u>.

If you find yourself doubting that this will make a difference, we recommend that you gather the items that the Holy Spirit brings to your attention, bag them up, and put them out in your garage or yard as a test. You will soon see and feel a difference in your home, as confirmation that this concept is true and real.

When you start the cleansing process, ask the Holy Spirit to lead you to the objects that need to go. He will then give you sensitivity to discern and also often lead you to things you did not even know you had.

Sometimes you will not be sure whether you should get rid of something or not. You may even sense that you should get rid of something, but you cannot understand why that would be. These are things to put in a bag and take out of the house. Once your house is completely clean and you feel that peace and light that was missing from your home, THEN after a season, you can bring those things back into your home one by one. As you do this, you will be able to test to see if the peace remains - or not.

Our simple motto is: IF IN DOUBT, THROW IT OUT!

To our way of thinking, there is nothing material in this world that is worth keeping at the expense of having the demonic harass and torment us or our children.

Thank You, Father, for leading us to this knowledge. Help those who begin this journey to listen to Your Holy Spirit's leading them to freedom in cleansing their homes of strongholds of the enemy. Give them the grace they need in order to obey You.

<u>S</u>

WHAT, WHY, & HOW TO CLEANSE YOUR HOME

"When you enter the land which the Lord your God gives you, you shall not learn to imitate the detestable things of those nations. There shall not be found among you anyone who makes his son or his daughter pass through the fire, one who uses divination, one who practices witchcraft, or one who interprets omens, or a sorcerer, or one who casts a spell, or a medium (one who consults familiar spirits), or a spiritist, or one who calls up the dead. For whoever does these things is detestable to the Lord, and because of these detestable things, the Lord your God will drive them out before you. You shall be blameless before the Lord your God. For those nations, which you shall dispossess, listen to those who practice witchcraft and to diviners, but as for you, the Lord your God has not allowed you to do so." <u>Deuteronomy 18:9-14</u>

Some of the following are items that will actually attract demonic activity and give demonic forces a point of connection (meaning - license or legal right) to enter your home and/or life. Some are items that simply do not bring glory to Jesus Christ.

The MAIN THING is to ask the Lord to help you, and His Holy Spirit will be faithful to guide you to everything that is in your home that should not be.

Again, when you find these articles, ideally they should be burned, if at all possible (based on the verse below). If they cannot be burned, then smash them and dispose of them.

"Many also of those who had believed kept coming, confessing, and disclosing their practices. And many of those who practiced magic brought their books together and began burning them in the sight of everyone; and they counted up the price of them and found it fifty thousand pieces of silver. So the word of the Lord was growing mightily and prevailing." <u>Acts 19:18-19</u>

<u>Note</u>: The below lists are not exhaustive. There are many other similar items that are not listed.

Note: I used to list specific name brands but do not find that wise in today's world to do that in a book. However, if you would like specific names of items that we have found to bring demonic infiltration into the home, I would be happy to send you that list upon request via email.)

ATTIRE containing things like skulls, dragons, swear words, ungodly slogans with wrong concepts, anything that represents death (mummies, bloody figures, etc.), immoral or ungodly concepts in picture form; possibly paisley prints (paisley originated as an expression of the essence of Zoroastrianism); all new age, false religion, and/or antichrist symbols, etc.

BOOKS containing: witchcraft, vampires, spells, sorcery, etc.; false doctrines (e.g. gifts are not for today, Christians cannot have demons, there is no hell, etc.); new age or humanistic philosophies; immoral acts or speech; even so-called Christian books that have been infiltrated by worldly philosophies.

GAMES AND TOYS
- Anything that glorifies sinful acts, practices, or people.
- Games and toys that children obsess over.
- Anything that has mythical or witchcraft like creatures or fixtures.
- Anything that contains immorality.

MOVIES AND TV
Good or bad, TV teaches our children. In many children's shows there are subliminal messages and adult themes, even in cartoons. It is highly recommended that you watch children's shows WITH your children, so that you are fully aware of what is in each show and accordingly adjust what you allow or sometimes even encourage your children to watch.)
- Anything that has to do with wizards, demons, ghosts, etc.
- Horror movies.
- Anything that makes light of ungodly themes such as adultery, fornication, drunkenness, homosexuality,

mockery of parents, fathers are idiots, mothers dominate the home, etc.

Note: *PLUGGED IN* (by *Focus on the Family*) is a good resource for finding out what a movie's content is from a Christian standpoint – <u>before</u> we view and/or purchase it. We have no excuse for "being surprised" at the content of any movie.

JEWELRY
- Anything connected with the occult, new age or other religions, peace signs, etc.
- Beware of crosses. Not all crosses are Christian.
- Anything from other countries, especially jewelry that stands for or is connected with the religious practices of that country.

KNICK-KNACKS
- Souvenirs from other countries, especially those connected with the religious practices of that country
- Collections of anything that becomes an idol
- Dragons
- Frogs (abomination to the Lord)
- Good luck charms, horseshoes used for luck, etc.
- Halloween items
- Incense (if connected to Eastern or other false religions)
- Indian artifacts (Kachina dolls, dream catchers, etc.)
- Items/Statues/Carvings/Pictures of things that other countries worship
- Kitchen Witch
- Mexican sun gods
- Owls (tied to occult and have been known in some instances to be linked to cancer in the home)
- Picture of Jesus with white hood (use Holy Spirit discernment with pictures of anything)
- Pictures of movie stars
- Shamrocks
- Tribal masks

- Unicorns (pray about, some ties to New Age symbolism, currently as of 2019 a new "obsession" with some people)
- Etc.

MISCELLANEOUS
- Alcohol (According to Proverbs 20:1 alcohol can bring spirit of mockery or arguing, fighting, and/or violence.)
- Areas where you have pictures of dead relatives
- Crystals
- Drug paraphernalia
- Essential Oils (of New Age origin – know your source)
- Horoscope, Numerology, Astrology (Deuteronomy 4:19)
- Letters, pictures, etc. from ex-girlfriends/boyfriends
- Pornography
- Yoga paraphernalia
- Etc.

MUSIC
- We recommend watching *They Sold Their Souls for Rock & Roll* or *Hell's Bells*, available at Amazon to rent or purchase.
- There are many musical groups and musicians that are known to be demon-possessed and/or tap into the occult to make their music, including having the words and music channeled to them from the dark side. Many have literally sold their souls to Satan in order to be successful. We highly recommend your getting rid of all music from musicians who are known to have done this and repent of your involvement with this music, even though you may not have known it was evil.
- Generally, if you really listen to the lyrics of the songs, it is easy to tell if they glorify God - or Satan and the flesh. After you have repented, ask the Lord to take back the ground that you gave to the enemy, and break the strongholds from your soul.
- Note: Remember to ask the Lord to cancel wrong words you have sung over yourself or others through the years, as the Holy Spirit brings them to mind.

SOME EXPLANATIONS FOR CLEANSING YOUR HOME OF ENEMY STRONGHOLDS

Idols: *"The graven images of their gods you shall burn with fire, you shall not desire the silver or gold that is on them, nor take it for yourself, lest you be ensnared by it; for it is an abomination to the Lord your God. Neither shall you bring an abomination (an idol) into your house, lest you be ensnared by it; for it is an abomination to the Lord your God."* Deuteronomy 7:25-26

Incense: Be careful with where your incense originates. Some of it is made (and sold) by cults.

Music: Watch *They Sold Their Souls for Rock and Roll* or *Hell's Bells* (both available on Amazon for rent or purchase).

Objects/Books from false religions: Demons are definitely attracted by objects and literature that pertain to false religions, cults, witchcraft in all forms, and Satanism. If at all possible, all such material should be burned (and do not be surprised if it does not burn easily) or otherwise destroyed.

Owls and Frogs: These are classified among the creatures mentioned in Deuteronomy 14:7-19 as being unclean and abominable. Owls are also frequently used in occult religions including Shamanism, Native Americans, witchcraft, sorcery, etc. Owls are also the major symbol of the Bohemian Club, and the demon goddess Lilith is shown as an owl.

Peace Signs: Trace the origin of peace signs.

Signs and Symbols: Be sure you know what signs and symbols represent before endorsing them. On the internet, you can easily find a site that gives pictures of many different symbols, their origins, and their meanings. We must become familiar with the many signs and symbols that are being used for evil in our world today.

ADDITIONAL NOTES ON CLEANSING YOUR HOME OF ENEMY STRONGHOLDS

One cannot always say exactly how the enemy is using things to affect our homes/families. Sometimes we can only find out how we are being affected by getting rid of the objects in question.

There is another way you can have demons in your home and that is if they "ride in" on someone who visits. So if you are having activity, ask the Lord to reveal any object giving license. If after 24 hours nothing has been revealed, then simply command the demon(s) to leave your home and go to Jesus to be dealt with. They likely do not have license to be there and, if that is the case, they will leave instantly.

Yet another way to have demons in your home is if someone who lives in your home has demons. Often it will be a non-Christian (perhaps an unsaved spouse). In this case, you can ask the Lord on a daily basis to stop all demons at the door and not allow them to enter in with that person. This is generally an effective way to deal with the demons in someone you live with.

If the demons have a lot of license in the person with whom you live, not all of them may stay at the door. In this case, you can ask the Lord to bind any remaining demons and not allow them to manifest in any way. Also, ask Him to open that person's eyes to the truth of God. (See *Prayer for Unsaved Loved Ones* in appendix area.)

TESTIMONIES OF CLEANSING THE HOME
OF ENEMY STRONGHOLDS

Testimony 1: Cleansing The Home by 25-Year-Old Man: *I have a testimony of how getting rid of the Book of Mormon from my closet resulted in my Crohn's symptoms going away. I had this Book of Mormon in my closet to use when missionaries came to my door. I know other Christians that have Mormon or Jehovah Witness literature at home, so I didn't think anything of it. I recently had a flare-up of Crohn's disease, and it went away overnight after removing the Book of Mormon from my house.*

Testimony 2: *I finally had to tell my mom that we don't "do" Hello Kitty. My daughter has been SO much better, since we got rid of the few Hello Kitty items that she had. And people, it only takes ONE item. You are better off with NO Hello Kitty at all. Since getting rid of Hello Kitty, I feel free and I see a huge change in my daughter's behavior. It has changed our lives. I notice that people with Hello Kitty have big lust issues, whether they admit it or not.*

Testimony 3: Cleansing The Home by Author and Family: *We spiritually cleansed our home of strongholds many years ago. But it is not a once and done thing. We have to be alert to the spiritual realm and take note of a shift away from the normal (e.g. contention in the home, fear, unexplained noises, etc.). So one day I was downstairs, and I started hearing noises in my bedroom. At first, I didn't think anything of it, until it was brought to mind that there was no one home! Experience then told me that we had poltergeists, but I was surprised that they were in my husband and my bedroom, since we were always very careful about allowing anything of the enemy in. Yet long ago I had learned that wherever the "activity" is, that is also where the "license" is. So I prayed as I always do, "Lord, show me what is in my room that is giving the enemy license." Within 24 hours, I was sitting in my room sorting through my grocery coupons, and there on the back of one of them was a full-page advertisement from a psychic, with her picture, her phone number, and her promises of what you would receive if you went to see her. Again, because of experience, I knew this was the* *cause of the poltergeists and immediately got rid of the ad. That was the end of the poltergeists.*

Testimony 4: Cleansing the Home of Amber Teething Necklace by Young Christian Couple*: Wife: Our baby was teething and very miserable. I had heard about the amber teething necklace as a solution for the pain of teething and decided to give it a try. When my husband saw the necklace on our son, he immediately reacted through his gift of discernment and told me that I should take it off of our son because it was connected to witchcraft. I didn't believe him, and we even argued about it. I will add at this point, that once my husband brought it to my attention, the Holy Spirit continued letting me know that something was not right with it. But I still did not take it off. I defended the necklace because I was thinking there was no way it could have been connected to witchcraft. Then a day or two later, our baby came down with a fever of 103 degrees and was miserable. After that, I also got a fever! In retrospect, I was able to discern that I got the fever too because I was the one who put the necklace on our son – and probably also because I did not listen to my husband's discernment. Once I got the fever, I took the necklace off, renounced witchcraft, and took back the ground that was given to the enemy when I put it on our son. He has been totally fine ever since. He just got his second tooth without my even realizing it. He had little to no discomfort. Praise God!*

Testimony 5: *I was hospitalized for a week for severe head pain. After many tests and scans, the doctors could find nothing wrong with me. You recommended that we go through and cleanse our homes and you specifically mentioned the possibility of having Hello Kitty objects, since I have granddaughters. Sure enough, we had a lot of Hello Kitty items. I got rid of them right away and as soon as I did, the sharp head pain began dissipating and eventually disappeared.*

Testimony 6: Cleansing The Home by 45-Year-Old Single Mom: *A few years back, during our Bible study for adults, we learned about cleansing our houses and removing all items that Satan might have an attachment to. We were even provided a list of things we might have in our house that needed to go. I found it an* *interesting study, but I wasn't exactly moved to go home and start tossing things out. However, a few months later, my house started to systematically fall apart. Lights were blowing out for no reason, the doorknobs were falling off, and the topper was the flood in my son's bathroom when we weren't home that caused a lot of damage to his room and the garage below. Plus, the mood in the house was just awful. It seemed that every time we came home we were constantly arguing at the tops of our lungs, most of the time over absolutely nothing. It wasn't your normal teen vs. adult arguing, if that's what you're thinking. It was much worse. I don't think either one of us was very happy there. Also, my son (now age 12) had always been afraid to be in our house. Every night he had a ritual to check all the doors and windows and look in all the closets and under all the beds for something hiding there. Not sure exactly what it was he feared, but no matter what I said, he always checked these places before bedtime. It didn't help that our dogs would start barking and howling nightly while we were trying to sleep. Not sure of what they were barking at, but they sure were bothered by whatever it was they were seeing or hearing.*

By this time we were going to the home church and the subject of cleansing our houses came up again. I was still skeptical, but decided that just as an experiment I would toss things that I thought might have some Satanic attachment and see what happened. What did have to lose anyway? I kind of had an idea in my mind of what to look for, especially since we had previously received a list during the first study. I started in my son's room one night, and by the end of the week I had either thrown out or burned probably 10 Hefty trash bags full of belongings. The funny thing was that the Lord seemed to lead me towards things that needed to go. For instance, my son's room was still torn up from the flood at this time and all his stuff was crammed into one side of the room. It was very difficult to see what was there much less what to throw out. However, the Lord led me to different spots in the room where I would immediately find things that needed to go. As an example, one night as I sat in my son's room, I heard the words, "don't forget the poster." Well, my son's room had no posters in it, so I had to wonder what that even meant, but it wasn't long before the Lord led me to my son's closet and there, shoved way in the back, was a framed poster of Pokémon characters that I had framed a long time ago and never hung up in his room.

During that week, I also started to notice some things. For one, my son wasn't doing his nighty ritual where he checked for whatever might be hiding in the house. When I asked him why he felt safer, he said he didn't really know why. Also, the bad mood in the house seemed to have lifted a lot. We weren't arguing and screaming as much. It has been that way ever since and my home has become one of my very favorite places to go.

Now I'm going to fast forward to today and let you know what has happened since that time. When I first told Sue about my experience with cleansing the house, she said the cleansing would happen in layers. I didn't really understand this concept, until now. After the initial cleansing of my house, the Lord would continue to lead me to items that I knew just by looking at them needed to go. We also became able to discern when something came into the house that had satanic attachments to it. For example, one day we rented a video that someone had recommended. When we watched it, it was absolutely evil, and we pulled the tape out within the first minutes of the movie. However, as the video sat there in its cover, my son and I knew the tape had to be returned right then, because we got such bad feelings from it. So, even though it was 11:00 at night, we jumped in the car just to return the tape.

Every once in a while I still find more things to throw out, which I find amazing since I started cleansing the house over two years ago. In fact, just this week I found Pokémon invitations left over from my son's 9th birthday party in one of the kitchen drawers, a drawer I had already cleaned out. So, obviously, the cleansing is an ongoing process.

In closing, I'm going to ask all of you to commit to something. I urge you to take the list you receive tonight and just as I did, make it an experiment to throw out even just the things on the list that you have in your house. Believe me, they aren't worth the money you paid for them. I guarantee that the Lord will lead you to all the items He wants you to get rid of, and in return, you will receive peace in your household and in your relationships there.

For the teens and kids here tonight, you can help with this too. There are probably things you know of that are not on the list since you are cooler than we adults are. So here are some guidelines for you to decide what you might want to throw out. If there are songs on your iPod or in your CD collection that you wouldn't feel comfortable listening to with Jesus at your side, then maybe it is time to get rid of them. If you wouldn't feel comfortable wearing certain clothing or jewelry in front of Jesus, then maybe it is time for you to stop wearing them. If you wouldn't say, "Hey, Jesus, come play this video game with me" or "let's watch this cool movie together," maybe it is time to stop playing that game or watching that movie. I think you get the idea. Anyway, pray for the Lord and the Holy Spirit to lead you, and He will. I truly pray that you'll try this and I'm excited to hear your stories about what happens when you cleanse your own homes and lives.

PRAYER TO CLEANSE YOUR HOME
AND CAST OUT DEMONS

After all ungodly objects have been removed from your home, modify this prayer to fit for whatever area you have jurisdiction over.

Note: No one has greater authority to pray over your home than those who live there, and most of all - the husband/father. If there is no husband/father in the home, then the head of household can do this. In the case where this is a woman, I would encourage asking a Christian grandfather or other male relative/male spiritual covering to join you as you pray, especially if you have known demonic activity.

Father, in Jesus' name, I take the authority over this home and land that You have given as a blessing to my family and me. I first of all repent of knowingly or unknowingly allowing objects into this home that gave the enemy license to come in. I specifically repent for (Let the Holy Spirit Guide You)_____
_____. *I ask for and receive Your forgiveness and thank You for Your grace and mercy over this family.*

I also choose to stand in the gap for those who owned this house and this land before we did. I confess, repent of, and ask Your forgiveness for all sins that were committed here. Specifically, I repent of all sexual sins. I repent for any sins of abuse (sexual, physical, spiritual, verbal, and/or emotional). I repent of any murder or rituals that were performed on this ground or any blood that was shed. (Continue on as the Spirit leads, confessing any sins He brings to mind.)

I ask that You cleanse and cover this home and all of its contents with the blood of Jesus Christ. I consecrate this home and everything in it to You. I command all anti-Christ spirits to remove yourselves from this place and go to Jesus to be dealt with. You are forbidden to return or go anywhere else. This includes all spirits of lust, fornication, adultery, pornography, perversion, and homosexuality, (Continue to list any the Lord brings to mind…). *Father, we as a family claim that: by the wisdom You give us, this house will be built; by the understanding You give us, this house will be established; and by the knowledge You give us, the rooms will be filled with all precious and pleasant riches. We claim this ground as Holy Ground, consecrated to You and You alone.*

At some point along the way, you can use anointing oil to anoint the gateways (doors and windows) with oil, as an outward sign of consecrating your home to God. I personally apply the oil to the same areas that Israel applied the blood of the lamb (top and two sides). This is not necessary; it is just what I like to do. (See section on *Anointing Oils*.)

Thank You, Father. We ask that You seal everything done today with the blood of Jesus Christ. In His name we pray, Amen.

Note: If you only have jurisdiction over a room or even half of a room, then an added step is necessary. *Father, in Jesus' name, I ask that You cordon off my area of jurisdiction and forbid any demonic spirits of darkness to cross the line into my domain. I claim this area as Holy ground, consecrated to You. Send angels as needed to carry out this ordination on any spirits that are rebellious.*

ANOINTING OILS

These are just some of the anointing oils that are available. However, for deliverance purposes, any anointing oil will do the job – even plain olive oil.

Cassia

Cedars of Lebanon

Frankincense

Henna

Hyssop

Ketubah

King's Garments

Lily of the Valley

Myrrh

Pomegranate

Rose of Sharon

Spikenard

You can get oils online from Jerusalem at <u>Abba Oil</u>.

(Some of these are also now available on Amazon.)

WHAT ARE SOUL TIES?

"Soul ties" (sometimes also called "relationship bonds") is the term we will use to describe linkages in the spiritual realm between two people. Soul ties can be good (such as in marriage or special friendships – e.g. David and Jonathan) - or they can be bad (such as in fornication, adultery, homosexuality, incest, pornography, bestiality, etc.).

"Now it came about when he had finished speaking to Saul, that the soul of Jonathan was knit to the soul of David, and Jonathan loved him as himself. Saul took him that day and did not let him return to his father's house. Then Jonathan made a covenant with David because he loved him as himself. Jonathan stripped himself of the robe that was on him and gave it to David, with his armor, including his sword and his bow and his belt. So David went out wherever Saul sent him and prospered; and Saul set him over the men of war. And it was pleasing in the sight of all the people and also in the sight of Saul's servants." I Samuel 18:1-6

Soul ties can be formed by sexual intercourse because the Bible tells us that in this way the two become one flesh (whether married or not).

There are also soul ties that can be formed when you have relinquished control of yourself to another person to control your thinking and/or your actions. It is even possible that you, yourself, may be the controlling person. For example, sometimes parents will overly control their children (as opposed to Biblically training them) or try to control them after they have become adults.

Side note on this topic: Once your child becomes a young adult (age 12-13), you will see how well you have trained him, because you will reap what you have sown. Pray that your children will bear fruits of the Spirit, but whatever the case, at that point, it is too late for you to control their actions and they will resent you if you try to. Bottom line: Train your children when they are young, so that when they are old, they will not depart from God's ways. See Proverbs 22:6.

SUMMARY OF TWO TYPES OF SOUL TIES

SEXUAL

- Includes: adultery, bestiality, cybersex, incest, fornication, homosexuality, molestation, perversion, pornography, etc.

  "...but from the beginning of creation, God made them male and female. For this reason a man shall leave his father and mother, <u>and the two shall become one flesh</u>; so they are no longer two, but one flesh." <u>Mark 10:6-7</u>

  "...or do you not know that the one who joins himself to a prostitute is <u>one body with her</u>? For he says, "the two shall become one flesh." <u>I Corinthians 6:16</u>

NON-SEXUAL

- Relationships with controlling people and/or organizational leaders (including church leaders) who are held in higher esteem than God Himself in your life.

- Anyone with whom you have been involved in illicit, immoral, and/or illegal activities of a non-sexual nature (e.g. drug use together, crime together, etc.). We know the Bible says in <u>I Corinthians 15:33</u> *"...bad company corrupts good morals."* So as an extra measure of precaution, we need to break soul ties with anyone who was bad company for us at any time in our lives. Be Spirit-led in this.

- Anyone or anything that you idolize, including Hollywood stars, rock stars, famous athletes, etc.

- The Lord also revealed to me that a Christian can have a soul tie with a tattoo parlor if he has a tattoo. I assume the soul tie is formed because the person has allowed another person to "let blood" from them. Life is in the blood. Therefore, there may be an unhealthy bond between the person that let the blood and the person who allowed the letting of the blood.

TATTOOS & SOUL TIES: FOOD FOR THOUGHT

<u>Leviticus 19:28</u> *"You shall not make any cuts in your body for the dead <u>nor</u> make any tattoo marks on yourselves: I am the LORD."*

<u>I Corinthians 6:19</u> *"Or do you not know that your body is a temple of the Holy Spirit who is in you, whom you have from God, and that you are not your own?"*

<u>I Corinthians 3:16-17</u> *"Do you not know that you are a temple of God and that the Spirit of God dwells in you? If any man destroys the temple of God, God will destroy him, for the temple of God is holy, and that is what you are."*

IN THINKING MORE ABOUT TATTOOS

- Are tattoos on our "temples" like graffiti on a church building?

- Is tattooing the same as bloodletting?
  http://www.av1611.org/tattoos/blood.html

MANY OF YOU ALREADY HAVE TATTOOS. THERE IS NO CONDEMNATION IN CHRIST JESUS. However, it is very important that you break off soul ties with the tattoo artist, cancel agreements made with the enemy in the process, and repent of all sinful attitudes or actions that led you to getting the tattoos to begin with (e.g. drunkenness, rebellion, etc.). See prayer below.

HOW TO DEAL WITH SOUL TIES

- Begin by making a list of those you have soul ties with. (It is good to include anyone you had a strong connection with, if it was unhealthy at any point in your relationship. Look for those who were able to control you more than you wished.)
  - Include relationships where there was sexual sin at any level.
  - Include relationships with controlling people, including church and other leaders who were held in too high esteem.
  - Include tattoo parlors and those who did the tattoos (blood-letting).
  - Include those you have idolized (including celebrities).
  - Include those with whom you were involved in illicit activities.

- Then go down the list one by one using *Prayer to Break Soul Ties*. It is important to be thorough with each person, because you are setting him/her free too.

- NOTE: When helping others to break soul ties, be sure you have built a level of trust with the individual FIRST. This can be a sensitive and potentially embarrassing subject for someone to share with another person.

MAKE YOUR PERSONAL SOUL TIE LIST BELOW
Use extra paper, as needed.

Sexual Soul Ties

Non-Sexual Soul Ties

PRAYER TO BREAK SOUL TIES

For Soul Ties Related to Tattoos

Father, in Jesus name, I repent of all sinful actions and attitudes that led me to getting this tattoo. (Confess what those sinful actions and attitudes were.) *I also ask that You break all soul ties that were formed between me and the person who did and the place where I got my tattoos. I cancel and renounce every ungodly thing that this tattoos stands for* (confess what that is specifically). *And I announce that there is One True God, the Creator of Heaven and Earth, whose son Jesus Christ of Nazareth shed His blood and died on the cross for my sins, so that through my repenting of my sins and choosing Him over all other gods, I am now a Son/Daughter of God who will live with Him eternally in Heaven. With that blood, I ask, Jesus, that You would cleanse and heal me from any defilement of the enemy over my body and soul through my actions. I ask that You now use this tattoo, Lord, to bring honor and glory to Your name and Your name alone! And with this anointing oil, I place a cross over this tattoo to symbolically dedicate it now to You, Lord Jesus. Amen.*

For Sexual Soul Ties: *Father, in Jesus name, I confess and repent of my sin of* (name the sexual intimacy) *with* (name of person). *I repent and ask for Your forgiveness.*

OR

For Non-Sexual Soul Ties: *Father, in Jesus name, I confess and repent of my sin of allowing* (name of person) *to have too much control over my thoughts, intents, and actions. I repent of and ask Your forgiveness for having any other god or idol before You. I declare that I will make You number one in my life above ALL others.*

THEN CONTINUE ON...

I ask that You take back the ground that was given to the enemy in my relationship with (name of person) *when* (list the remembrances that the Holy Spirit brings to mind), *and I ask that You break every stronghold from my soul.*

By an act of my will, I choose to forgive (name of person) *for all of these things. I also choose to forgive myself. And I ask that You give me Your grace to do so.*

I ask that You sever all soul ties between (name of person) *and me. Return to him the pieces of his soul that stayed with me. Return to me the pieces of my soul that stayed with him.*

I ask that You bind the enemy from (Name of Person); *take off all the veils of the enemy; and open his eyes, ears, heart, and soul to the truth of God. I also ask that You bring someone to him who can lead him to salvation.* (And then release that person to God as if he were a helium balloon. You are done with that person and he is in God's hands now – and out of yours! Do not allow yourself to focus on memories of this person any longer.)

(Do the above with each person you have sexual and nonsexual soul ties with. After you have prayed through each one thoroughly, then pray the final prayer below.)

FINAL CLOSING PRAYER

Jesus, I ask that You call to Your hands the pieces of my soul that are returning to me, cleanse and heal them with Your blood, bring them to my current age, and integrate them back into my soul where they split off – so that it will be as though that never happened.

Cleanse my body inside and out with the blood of Jesus, so that the defilement of the enemy will be completely removed from me.

Fill me up afresh with Your Holy Spirit in every place vacated by the enemy.

DEALING WITH LUST

(All verses for this topic are printed out on the page titled *Some Verses On Lust*.)

First and foremost, we must understand that while lust does major damage to husbands and wives in marriage and deeply affects relationships within the family, more than anything else:

LUST IS A MATTER OF THE HEART
BETWEEN MAN (or WOMAN) AND GOD.

FACTS ABOUT LUST

- Lust is one area where Satan is the most successful. Using the opposite sex is one of his easiest and most effective weapons.

- Lust is an area where failure will result in more failure (in the family, business, church, etc.).

- If husbands do not honor their wives, their prayers will be hindered. (I Peter 3:7)

- The battle is in your mind. If you give in there, the battle moves to actions and at that point strongholds are started, and forces of the enemy are then able to attach to and operate from these strongholds. (Possible demonic attachments include spirits of lust, addiction, fornication, adultery, perversion, pedophilia, incest, homosexuality, bestiality, etc. You can tell which demons have attached by what you struggle with.)

- Human eyes are never satisfied. (Proverbs 27:20) Therefore, if lust is not stopped, there will be a progression into increasingly perverse forms of sexual sin. Note: We are seeing more & more men and women having extramarital affairs, & there has been a marked increase in cross-dressing and gender change.

- More women than ever also now struggle with lust. Because the spirit of lust has been "fed" more and more over the years, the U.S. now has strong ruling powers of lust over it. Even women are joining their men in viewing pornography, rather than resisting this sin and standing for Godly purity.

- Jesus never lusted. (Hebrews 4:14-16) Therefore, we know that there must to be a way to gain victory over lust!

THE STARK REALITIES OF WHAT THE BIBLE SAYS ABOUT LUST

- Looking at a woman with lust = Adultery. (Matthew 5:27-28)

- Those who practice adultery and fornication will not inherit the kingdom of God. (Galatians 5:19-21)
  - o Note: This was written to The Church.
  - o Question: So what does this verse mean?

- Proverbs 7 teaches us how a seductress operates and the consequences of involvement with her, including liver damage (verse 23). A "seductress" is any woman that seduces…not just a prostitute.
  - o She is considered a stranger.
  - o She flatters with her words.
  - o She catches those who lack sense.
  - o She catches the youth.
  - o She catches the naïve.
  - o Her ways are cloaked by night and darkness.
  - o She dresses like a prostitute.
  - o She is cunning of heart.
  - o She is boisterous.
  - o She is rebellious.
  - o She does not remain at home.
  - o She is out and about on the streets.
  - o She is brazen.
  - o She entices.
  - o She is persuasive.
  - o She seduces.
  - o Giving in to her can cause liver damage.
  - o Giving in to her will cost you your life.
  - o Her paths will lead you to death.

YOU MUST BE INTENTIONAL IN OVERCOMING LUST

- It is important that you **break all strongholds and soul ties and get rid of all demonic spirits**. See: *Prayers to Break All Forms of Lust*. It is recommended you then do the below as you "walk out your freedom in Christ."

- Upon awakening, **ask God for His Grace** to overcome all temptations of the enemy. Remember: Grace = God gives us His desire and His power to do His will. (II Corinthians 12:9) See prayer under *Daily Hygiene to Overcome Lust*.

- Know that you need to **take every thought captive**. (II Corinthians 10:3-5) If we do not take our thoughts captive, Satan will take our thoughts captive. And he holds those thoughts in darkness and then uses them to manipulate you into further sin and secrecy.

- **Confess your sins one to another**. In this case, you are to confess your sins to your spouse. (James 5:16) Note: *Sorry, but I do not see accountability between men working AT ALL!*

- **Fear God**! God is always watching, and He will chasten. Do not think you are getting away with this sin just because God is longsuffering. Know that you will reap what you sow.

- **Remind yourself** that those who practice sexual sin of any kind are in danger of Hell fire. (Galatians 5:19-21)

- **Know** that your practice of sin will cause you to not only lose fellowship with God, but it will seer your conscience and start a downward spiral in your life that will cause you to be handicapped in discerning right from wrong or good from evil.

- **Love your wife**. (Ephesians 5:25-33)

- **Love your family**. It is extremely important for men to know that as the spiritual leader and covering over your home, your participation in acts of immorality will affect your children.

Your children will struggle with lust, they may be attacked by demonic forces of lust (Incubus/Succubus), and/or the enemy will have freedom to bring circumstances where they will see or hear things that are immoral – and quite often, things that are way too advanced for their minds to comprehend and handle.

- **Flee from immorality (in your mind and your body)!** (I Corinthians 6:18-20)

- **Read Proverbs 5, 6, 7** which will give you: signs to watch for, consequences of this kind of sin that will helpfully motivate you to stay away from it, and some instruction on how to avoid this sin.

- **Know that you are not alone.** (I Corinthians 10:13)

- **Know that God will provide a way of escape.** (I Corinthians 10:13-14)

- **Break bondage by fasting**. (Isaiah 58:6)

- **Pray to break new strongholds of lust daily**, if necessary. This should be done anytime you fall into lust with your eyes and mind.

- **Meditate on the Word of God and use the Word as a weapon against the enemy**.

- **Purpose not to defile yourself**. (I Corinthians 6:18-20, Daniel 1:8)

- **Make a covenant with your eyes**, as Job did. (Job 31:1)

- **Pray for the salvation of the ones the enemy tries to entice you with** – every time he entices you. Satan hates this! (Romans 12:21)

- **When pictures come to mind**, use them as a springboard to picture Jesus on the cross, dying for that sin. Do not look at the porn that comes to your mind from the past.

INSTRUCTION FOR WOMEN

- Know that your man struggles with lust, even if you do not think he does.

- Choose family entertainment (including movies, shows, gym, swimming areas, etc.) where your man will not be tempted to lust.

- Pray for the men in your life (including your pastors and leaders).

- Dress modestly. (Ask the men in your life if you are being modest.)

- Be grateful if you have a husband who cares to work on this.

- Respect your husband! (Ephesians 5:33)

- If your husband fails, work together to find solutions. Be solution-oriented - not problem-oriented

- Show your husband the Grace of God (Grace = God operating through you to give you the desire and the power to do His will.) It is God's will that you show your husband respect, even when he fails.

SOME VERSES ON LUST

Job 31:1 *"I have made a covenant with my eyes; how then could I gaze at a virgin?"*

Proverbs 5, 6, 7 Read these chapters in your Bible.

Proverbs 27:20 *"Sheol and Abaddon are never satisfied, nor are the eyes of man ever satisfied."*

Isaiah 58:6 *"Is this not the fast which I choose, too loosen the bonds of wickedness, to undo the bands of the yoke, and to let the oppressed go free and break every yoke?"*

Daniel 1:8 *"But Daniel made up his mind that he would not defile himself..."*

Matthew 5:27-28 *"You have heard that it was said, 'You shall not commit adultery,' but I say to you that everyone who looks at a woman with lust for her has already committed adultery with her in his heart."*

Romans 12:21 *"Do not be overcome by evil but overcome evil with good."*

I Corinthians 6:18-20 *"Flee from sexual immorality. All other sins a person commits are outside the body, but whoever sins sexually, sins against their own body. Do you not know that your bodies are temples of the Holy Spirit, who is in you, whom you have received from God? You are not your own; you were bought at a price. Therefore, honor God with your bodies."*

I Corinthians 7:1-5 *"Now concerning the things about which you wrote, it is good for a man not to touch a woman. But because of immoralities, each man is to have his own wife, and each woman is to have her own husband. The husband must fulfill his duty to his wife, and likewise also the wife to her husband. The wife does not have authority over her own body, but the husband does; and likewise also the husband does not have authority over his own body, but the wife does. Stop depriving one another, except by agreement for a time, so that you may devote yourselves to prayer, and come together again so that Satan will not tempt you because of your lack of self-control."*

I Corinthians 10:13-14 *"No temptation has overtaken you, but such as is common to man; and God is faithful, who will not allow you* to be tempted beyond what you are able, but with the temptation will provide the way of escape also, so that you will be able to endure it. Therefore, my Beloved, flee from idolatry."

II Corinthians 10:3-5 "For though we walk in the flesh, we do not war according to the flesh, for the weapons of our warfare are not of the flesh, but divinely powerful for the destruction of fortresses. We are destroying speculations and every lofty thing raised up against the knowledge of God, and we are taking every thought captive to the obedience of Christ..."

II Corinthians 12:9 "And He has said to me, 'My grace is sufficient for you, for power is perfected in weakness.' Most gladly, therefore, I will rather boast about my weaknesses, so that the power of Christ may dwell in me."

Galatians 5:19-21 "Now the deeds of the flesh are evident, which are: immorality, impurity, sensuality, idolatry, sorcery, enmities, strife, jealousy, outbursts of anger, disputes, dissensions, factions, envying, drunkenness, carousing, and things like these, of which I forewarn you, just as I have forewarned you, that those who practice such things will not inherit the kingdom of God."

Ephesians 5:25-33 "Husbands, love your wives, just as Christ also loved the church... and gave Himself up for her, so that He might sanctify her, having cleansed her by the washing of water with the word, so that He might present Himself to the church in all her glory, having no spot or wrinkle or any such thing; but that she would be holy and blameless. So, husbands ought also to love their own wives as their own bodies. He who loves his own wife loves himself; for no one ever hated his own flesh, but nourishes and cherishes it, just as Christ also does the church, because we are members of His body. For this reason a man shall leave his father and mother and shall be joined to his wife, and the two shall become one flesh. This mystery is great; but I am speaking with reference to Christ and the church. Nevertheless, each individual among you also is to love his own wife even as himself, and the wife must see to it that she respects her husband."

<u>Hebrews 4:14-16</u> *"Therefore, since we have a great high priest who has passed through the heavens, Jesus the Son of God, let us hold fast our confession. For we do not have a high priest who cannot sympathize with our weaknesses, but One who has been tempted in all things as we are, yet without sin. Therefore, let us draw near with confidence to the throne of grace, so that we may receive mercy and find grace to help in time of need."*

<u>James 5:16</u> *"Therefore, confess your sins one to another, and pray for one another so that you may be healed. The effective prayer of a righteous man can accomplish much."*

<u>II Timothy 2:22</u> *"Flee the evil desires of youth and pursue righteousness, faith, love and peace, along with those who call on the Lord out of a pure heart."*

<u>I Peter 3:7</u> *"You husbands in the same way, live with your wives in an understanding way, as with someone weaker, since she is a woman; and show her honor as a fellow heir of the grace of life, so that your prayers will not be hindered."*

PRAYER TO BREAK ALL FORMS OF LUST
Make sure soul ties are broken first.
(See *What are Soul Ties?*)

The following prayers are a guide but listen to the Holy Spirit because He will often add more. Be led by Him because He knows things you could not possibly know, especially about where the roots of these things started in past generations. Whatever comes to mind, ask the Lord to break it off of you, even if it may seem strange. Better to ask to break something that is not there, than to miss something that is there - just because we have no proof.

Father, in Jesus' name, I repent of having viewed pornography, participating in cyber sexual fantasies...(list others.) *I ask for Your forgiveness and by an act of my will I choose to turn from my wicked ways, and I ask that You give me Your grace to do so.*

I ask that You take back all of the ground that was given to the enemy when I did these things (be as specific with the times and incidents as the Lord brings to your mind*) and break every stronghold from my soul.*

I also choose to stand in the gap for my forefathers who participated in acts of lust and perversion including pornography, homosexuality, bestiality, (list any others that the Holy Spirit brings to mind). *I repent on their behalf and ask for Your forgiveness. I renounce lust. I renounce perversion.* (Continue renouncing by name.) *And I ask that You sever every generational cord of iniquity from me and all future generations.*

I ask, Father, in Jesus' name, that You would cancel every spell and every curse spoken over me by my forefathers. I ask that You cancel every spell and every curse attached to any pictures or sites that I have viewed. I also ask that You break all soul ties between me and any person or even picture that I have lusted over.

I renounce pornography. I renounce addiction. I renounce self-love. I renounce low self-esteem. (Continue renouncing by name including lust, perversion, homosexuality, immorality, sodomy, fornication, adultery, masturbation, bestiality, voyeurism, cybersex, orgies, etc.)

I come boldly to Your throne of Grace, Lord, asking for an extra measure of Your Grace to overcome all spirits of lust and every temptation of the flesh and the eyes. Give me Your Grace to turn away instantly and to flee from temptation as Your Word tells me to do. (Memorize Biblical verses as the Holy Spirit gives them to you and use those verses as weapons against the enemy.)

And I command any spirits of pornography, addiction, lust, self-love, perversion, homosexuality, immorality, sodomy, fornication, adultery, masturbation, bestiality, voyeurism, cybersex, orgies, etc. to leave me now, in the name of Jesus Christ. You are to go to Jesus to be dealt with and you are forbidden to return to me. (<u>Note</u>: You can do this yourself, or you can ask a trusted Christian brother (if a man) or sister (if a woman) and he/she can lay hands on you and pray along with you as you do these commands.)

Wash me now with the blood of Jesus Christ, inside and outside, removing all of the defilement of the enemy over me. Bless me now with purity of heart, mind, and soul; a single-minded focus on You; self-control; the willingness and power to be a one-woman-man/one-man-woman; the ability to know and demonstrate true love as Christ loves His bride; and the ability to be the man/woman of God you created me to be in all areas of my life, especially as a husband/wife and father/mother, son/daughter, or brother/sister.

And give me a fresh filling of Your Holy Spirit, filling in all areas vacated by the enemy. Breathe the breath of life on all of the gifts and fruits of Your Holy Spirit that You have blessed me with.

DAILY HYGIENE TO OVERCOME LUST

First thing in the morning, pray: *"Father, In Jesus' name, I ask that You bind all Satanic forces from the highest to the lowest levels – from being able to affect those who are under my care or me today. I ask that You put us in complete isolation from the enemy so that nothing we say or do can be perceived by him. Bless us with a fresh filling of Your Holy Spirit and give us Your Grace to overcome every temptation."*

As soon as you feel even a little bit of lust, know that it is a Demon of Lust around you and speak the following (even in a whisper): *"Demon of Lust, I command you now in Jesus' name to be gone from me and go to Jesus to be dealt with."*

MINISTRY FOR ABORTION

Portions of the below are also useful for miscarriages, stillbirths, & childhood deaths

If you have had one or more abortions, miscarriages, stillbirths, or death of a child, it is recommended that you find someone to go through the below process with you. It is possible to do on yourself if you prefer. In either case, follow the below recommendations and steps.

Most people will only tell another person they have been involved in one or more abortions after they have assured themselves:

- That you are compassionate.
- That you are trustworthy and do not speak of private matters outside of the ministry room.
- That you are someone who does not shock easily.
- That you love unconditionally, just as Jesus does.
- That you exhibit the fact that there is no condemnation in Christ Jesus.
- That you have knowledge of the tools needed to help that person come to freedom.

As well, the ministry for abortion also needs to be available not only for the woman who had the abortion but also for:

- The <u>man</u> whose child was aborted (even if he is not sure it was his child).
- The <u>parents</u> who gave permission.
- The <u>friends</u> who assisted in some way (monetarily, driving the person, supporting the abortion, etc.).

At the least, these participants must repent for all sin they were involved in, including coming into agreement with murder.

STEPS OF MINISTRY

1. Repent for all known sin. This would include: *all sexual sin involved, murder, rebellion, playing God, selfishness, fear of man, etc.* Each situation will be slightly different, and you will want to help the person discern what sinful thoughts and actions took place surrounding his/her situation, so that these can be repented for.

2. Take back the ground, etc. using *Prayer to Break Strongholds.*

3. Have the person complete the following statement and write down the words he/she uses. "When I went through this abortion, it caused me to feel…"

4. Walk the person through forgiveness for all involved – especially self! See section on *Forgiveness.*

5. Ask the Lord to heal the person inside and outside with the blood of Jesus.

6. Cast off/out any spirits that may have attached (as led by the Holy Spirit). Note: These will likely include the above under Step #1 as well as the "feelings that were caused" which you listed under #3. This gives you a guide as to what spirits have likely attached.

7. Ask the person if she (or he) would like to know the sex of the child? If so, guide her in going before the Holy Spirit. Have her completely clear her mind and then ask the Lord what sex the child is. (Note: Allow the person to do this. You pray. You may confirm, if you get the same thing. But ultimately it is the person, him- or herself, who needs to hear from the Lord, in order for it to be real for him/her. If she is unable to hear, then send her home with the encouragement to keep asking and listening. The Lord may reveal the answer in a dream or in some other way. We serve a creative God.)

8.   Ask the person if she (or he) would like to know the name of the child? If so, guide her in going before the Holy Spirit. Have her completely clear her mind and then ask the Lord what name He has given to this child. (Note: Same as note in Step 7.)

    a. Instruct the mother or father of the child that his/her child will be among the first to greet them in Heaven. From now on, whenever they think of this child, it should be with excited anticipation of seeing that child in Heaven. No longer are they to look to the past…only to their future in Heaven together. *

* Note: Some have questioned whether a baby truly goes to Heaven. We say yes, based on the following:

- To go to Hell, one must reject Christ and His plan of salvation. A baby is obviously not able to do that.
- We do know that babies are in Heaven based on David's testimony in II Samuel 12:21-23 *"Then [David's] servants said to him, 'What is this thing that you have done? While the child was alive, you fasted and wept; but when the child died, you arose and ate food.' He said, 'While the child was still alive, I fasted and wept; for I said, "'Who knows, the LORD may be gracious to me, that the child may live.'" But now he has died; why should I fast? Can I bring him back again? I will go to him, but he will not return to me.'"*

ABORTION TESTIMONY

<u>ABORTION AT AGE 17</u> 25-year-old woman: *Although I was raised in a Christian home, I became sexually active at a very young age, losing my virginity at the age of 15. After years of unprotected sex with my boyfriend, the inevitable happened; I became pregnant. As a senior in high school with a large stack of college acceptance letters, I could see that my future seemed bright except for this one bump in the road. It's sad to admit, but at the time, I didn't really think twice about my decision. I just wanted the problem to go away. So, at 17 years old I had an abortion. Looking back now, I see how that seeming "quick-fix" had years of destructive consequences. In college, I became promiscuous and dabbled in drugs and binge drinking. Looking back, I can see that it was all a way to numb the deep pain in my heart. I lost my self-worth and believed the lie of the enemy that I had done the unforgiveable and that God didn't want me because I was a murderer. Years later when the Holy Spirit was leading me back to the Lord, I knew I had to deal with the decision from my past that haunted me. I embarked on a deliverance journey with two seasoned deliverance ministers and one of the first things I brought to light was my abortion. Just saying the word aloud made me burst into tears, but it was so healing to speak it out and not hide it any longer. One of the most healing moments I can remember is when my deliverance minister suggested that we ask the Lord specifics about my baby, like the gender or name. I was open to the idea because I knew that it was just another step in the healing process. I sat silently, cleared my head, and tried to concentrate on hearing that still small voice of truth. Almost immediately, I heard the name Matthew. After a few minutes one of my deliverance ministers confirmed that she had seen the color blue and the other asked me what color hair my boyfriend had. I said "black" and she started to cry as she shared with me the vision she had. She had seen Jesus holding my black-haired baby boy in his arms and said he was full of joy. It brought so much peace to my heart to know that he was in a better place and that I didn't need to worry about him. I was free to let go of the guilt and finally accept the forgiveness that Jesus paid for on the cross. For so long I didn't feel worthy of His forgiveness and I thought there was always*

152

going to be a block in my relationship with Him. By finding out specifics of my baby, I felt like the Lord was telling me that everything was alright and that He works all things out, for the good of those who love God and are called according to His purposes. (Romans 8:28) I was left in total awe that the God of the Universe would meet me in such an intimate and personal way and reveal things to bring love and healing to my heart. Knowing the gender and name of my baby helped me to view him as a human being and not just a clump of cells. In my mind, in order to justify such a horrible act as abortion, I had convinced myself that Matthew was nameless and faceless and possessed no life. Learning who he is and knowing that one day I'll meet him face to face in heaven was extremely powerful and a major step towards claiming my full freedom in Christ. And, by the way, the name Matthew means "Gift From God."

SUMMARY

Dear Brothers and Sisters,

Please continue reading through the appendices area, as there are tools contained in those pages that will be helpful not only for you, yourself, but also for others the Lord leads you to teach and minister to. (By the way, did you know that teaching is a <u>command of Christ</u> - as part of The Great Commission? (See <u>Matthew 28:16-20</u>.)

Once you have finished the appendices area, it will then be time for you to start your own walk to freedom. On the following pages, I have put together a worksheet for you to use to journal your progress. Please make as many copies of these worksheets as you need. My hope is that you will find them helpful in "covering all of the bases" with each stronghold that is broken off of your soul.

Onward Ho!

Appendix: <u>COMMANDS OF THE GREAT COMMISSION</u>
Our Marching Orders

PREACH
BAPTIZE IN WATER
BAPTIZE IN HOLY SPIRIT
TEACH JESUS' COMMANDS
MAKE DISCIPLES
SHOW SIGNS (below)
PROCLAIM REPENTANCE FOR FORGIVENESS OF SINS TO
ALL NATIONS

<u>SIGNS WHICH IDENTIFY TRUE BELIEVERS</u>
CAST OUT DEMONS
SPEAK WITH NEW TONGUES
DO DANGEROUS THINGS & NOT BE HURT
HEAL

<u>THE GREAT COMMISSION VERSES</u>

<u>Matthew 28:16-20</u> *"But the eleven disciples proceeded to Galilee, to the mountain, which Jesus had designated. 17 When they saw Him, they worshiped Him; but some were doubtful. 18 And Jesus came up and spoke to them, saying, 'All authority has been given to Me in heaven and on earth. 19 Go therefore and <u>make disciples</u> of all the nations, <u>baptizing them</u> in the name of the Father and the Son and the Holy Spirit, 20 <u>teaching them</u> to observe all that I commanded you; and lo, I am with you always, even to the end of the age.'"*

<u>Mark 16:14-18</u> *Afterward He appeared to the eleven themselves, as they were reclining at the table; and He reproached them for their unbelief and hardness of heart, because they had not believed those who had seen Him after He had risen. 15 And He said to them, "Go into all the world and <u>preach the gospel</u> to all creation. 16 He who has believed and has been baptized shall be saved; but he who has disbelieved shall be condemned. 17 These <u>signs</u> will accompany those who have believed: in My name they will <u>cast out demons</u>, they will <u>speak with new tongues</u>; 18 they will pick up*

155

serpents, and if they drink any deadly poison, it <u>will not hurt them</u>; they will <u>lay hands on the sick</u>, and they will recover."

<u>Luke 24:44-53</u> *Now He said to them, "These are My words which I spoke to you while I was still with you, that all things which are written about Me in the Law of Moses and the Prophets and the Psalms must be fulfilled." 45 Then He opened their minds to understand the Scriptures, 46 and He said to them, "Thus it is written, that the Christ would suffer and rise again from the dead the third day, 47 and that <u>repentance for forgiveness of sins would be proclaimed</u> in His name to all the nations, beginning from Jerusalem. 48 You are witnesses of these things. 49 And behold, I am sending forth the promise of My Father upon you; but you are to stay in the city until you are clothed with power from on high." 50 He led them out as far as Bethany, and He lifted up His hands and blessed them. 51 While He was blessing them, He parted from them and was carried up into heaven. 52 And they, after worshiping Him, returned to Jerusalem with great joy, 53 and were continually in the temple praising God.*

Appendix: <u>DELIVERANCE FAQs</u>

What is deliverance?

Deliverance, for our purposes, is the cleansing and healing of the <u>soul</u> after identifying and having Jesus break off the <u>strongholds</u>, <u>soul ties</u>, <u>generational iniquities</u>, and other attachments of the enemy in order for us to be able to claim the full freedom that Jesus died for.

What is the soul?

The soul, for our purposes, is the mind, will, and emotions. The will is all our own. The mind and the emotions, however, are where the enemy can build <u>strongholds</u> from which he can then operate to control and manipulate us.

What is a stronghold?

A stronghold by definition is a fortress. See <u>II Corinthians 10:3-5</u>. A stronghold can be good (God is our stronghold) or it can be bad (when it is a place from which the enemy operates.) With the deliverance process, we identify the roots causes of the strongholds and ask Jesus to take back all of the ground that has been given to the enemy and remove the strongholds from our souls.

What is a soul tie?

A soul tie, basically speaking, is an unhealthy connection with another person. This happens most frequently through fornication, but we will be exploring other possible ways an unhealthy soul tie can form between two people. (<u>I Corinthians 6:16</u>)

What are generational iniquities?

Generational iniquities are the sins of our forefathers that were passed down through the generations. (<u>Exodus 34:6-7</u>)

Did I receive Freedom in Christ at Salvation?

Yes, you did. But we live in a battle zone. And the instant you said, "I do," to Christ, something else kicked into action. That "something else" was the enemy – the devil and his minions. Prior to that point, you were not a threat. But the moment you joined

God's side, Satan and his minions went into high gear to steal that seed from you before it took root.

The Enemy has numerous ways to do that. See Matthew 13:18-23.

- Keeping you from understanding: He tries to bring confusion to you and keep true Believers away from you, so that you never really understand what you did in receiving Christ as your Savior, and therefore you are weakened in your ability to grow in your knowledge of Him and His ways. Eventually the enemy is able to snatch away the little bit of the Word that was sown into your heart.
- Bringing affliction and persecution: He tries to keep you from having the Word take root in your heart, by using people and situations to afflict you and persecute you because of your new faith, and you soon decide it is not worth what you are having to go through, so you walk away from the Word.
- Bringing distractions and making you think you need to have more money than you do: He keeps you busy and distracted, often with the goal of obtaining more wealth. As a result, the Word gets choked out, is unfruitful for you, and you forget about it.

The Enemy is only able to do the above for two reasons:

- You are not being discipled by a fellow Believer in Jesus Christ, who has been seasoned past this point, and therefore can walk beside you until you are able to see how to do this for yourself AND/OR
- You still have strongholds on your soul from which the Enemy can manipulate you through reminding you of your past sin, your past pain, and your inherited weaknesses (generational iniquities). (This is where the instruction in this book comes in to help you.)

This is why Christ tells us to make disciples in Matthew 28:19 *"Go therefore and make disciples of all the nations..."* and to *"work out [our] salvation with fear and trembling."* Philippians 2:12

As Children of God, we need to step up to the plate! It really is our responsibility to help new Believers learn the truths about the battle they have just entered by becoming one with Christ. It is not a cakewalk; it is a process...and, as we all know, it is not an easy process. Let's invest ourselves, as Sons and Daughters of God, into the lives of new Believers. (This book will help you to help other Christians claim their freedoms in Christ.)

How does one know when he is free in Christ?

You know you are free in Christ when you are able to live in the moment. No longer will the memories of the past haunt you or thoughts of the future cause you fear. No longer will you be self-focused on your problems and issues. You will be confident in who you are in Christ, and you will be able to go forward and help others, using whatever gifting God has given you. See John 8:36.

How do I know if my home has strongholds?

There are three primary ways you can tell if your home itself has strongholds: if you or someone in your home is fearful, is contentious, and/or has nightmares. There are actually also many other ways the enemy can affect your home and family, but often these ways go unrecognized and are considered "normal." These ways can include infirmities such as headaches, stomachaches, etc.; anxiety; lust; etc. You may not know how these strongholds are affecting your family until they are removed – and the manifestations cease.

What kind of things do I need to get rid of in order to get the strongholds out of my home?

See *Cleansing Your Home of Enemy Strongholds*.

How do I know if I need deliverance?

Everyone needs deliverance, but we only do deliverance on Christians, because they are the only ones who have the ability to have their "clean, empty rooms" filled up with the Holy Spirit. See Matthew 12:43-45.

Should we do deliverance on non-believers?

Generally speaking (99% of the time) – no. You can actually make things much worse for them! See Matthew 12:43-45. It is always much safer to have someone you are working with get to the point where they are willing to repent of their sins first. Once that has been done and he is filled with the Holy Spirit, he now has the ability to have any "rooms that are empty" then filled with the Holy Spirit of God.

Can a Christian have demons? (For more, see: *Can Christians Have Demons?*)

The answer to this question is – Yes, without a doubt! Anyone who is a seasoned deliverance minister will tell you the same thing. The Biblical term is actually the Greek word *daimonizomai,* which means to have an unclean spirit, to be under the power or influence of a demon, or to be vexed (meaning harassed, tormented, or troubled) with an evil spirit. Demons can oppress us on the outside and they can also live with us on the inside, if they have license to do so. That license is given to them through the strongholds that are on our souls, caused by generational iniquity, sin, and/or emotional wounding.

But how can light and darkness dwell together? (For more, see: *Can Christians Have Demons?*)

The quickest answer to this is – Was not Satan (dark) able to go to Jesus (light) and be right next to him? Matthew 4:1-11 Do not light and dark dwell side-by-side everywhere in the world? If dark and light were not dwelling together, we would not need a Savior.

I have never seen demons manifesting in Christians, so I do not believe it is possible.

We know from John 3:20 that demons hate the light: *"For everyone who does evil hates the Light, and does not come to the Light for fear that his deeds will be exposed."* If demons are with a person, they will often hide (like cockroaches) when around another true Christ-follower.

Do demons lie?

Generally speaking, demons definitely do lie to us in our everyday lives. But when demons manifest during a deliverance session, we have not found this to commonly be the case. Ask the Lord for discernment prior to the session, and if they do try to lie, you will likely be able to sense it in your Spirit. We believe the reason they rarely lie in the ministry room is because they can see Jesus with us (where two or three are gathered in My name...) and in the Bible there is no record of the demons lying when confronted by Jesus. All said, however, it would be wise as a precaution prior to starting a deliverance session to command the demons to tell the truth.

Should we allow demons to speak during a session?

Yes...and no. Yes, they can be asked questions as to what license they have and how they got there. But they should not be allowed to speak beyond that. You should always be in control of the session no matter what. The purpose of allowing the demonic to speak is merely to gain information that will help you to get them OUT!

If a demon manifests violently, what do I do? (For more, see: *When Casting Out Demons.*) Bind it, in the name of Jesus, and command it not to manifest until called upon to release. Regroup. Ascertain what license it has. Through cooperation with the person, remove the stronghold. Then unbind the demon and command it to come out and go to Jesus to be dealt with. (This is obviously a short version answer. You will learn more as you go through Levels 2 and 3 of *Deliverance For Christians.*)

Can all Christians do deliverance? ((For more, see: *When Casting Out Demons.*)

As born-again, Spirit-filled, Spirit-empowered Christians, we have been given the authority by Jesus to do what Jesus did while He was here on earth. That said, however, you must not carelessly move into this calling. First of all: Count the cost. *"For which one of you, when he wants to build a tower, does not first sit down and calculate the cost to see if he has enough to complete it?"* Luke 14:28

Secondly: You will need to grow in your authority, until the demonic recognizes that you are a Son/Daughter of God who carries His authority and power. This requires knowing Him, shedding all unrighteousness, and following after Him with your whole heart of obedience and surrender.

Appendix: <u>DELIVERANCE VERSES</u>

<u>CHRISTIANS NEED TO CLEANSE THEIR HOMES/PROPERTIES</u>

<u>Deuteronomy 7:25-26</u> *"You shall burn the carved images of their gods with fire; you shall not covet the silver or gold that is on them, nor take it for yourselves, lest you be snared by it; for it is an abomination to the LORD your God. Nor shall you bring an abomination into your house, lest you be doomed to destruction like it. You shall utterly detest it and utterly abhor it, for it is an accursed thing."*

<u>Deuteronomy 18:9-14</u> *"When you enter the land which the LORD your God gives you, you shall not learn to imitate the detestable things of those nations. There shall not be found among you anyone who makes his son or his daughter pass through the fire, one who uses divination, one who practices witchcraft, or one who interprets omens, or a sorcerer, or one who casts a spell, or a medium, or a spiritist, or one who calls up the dead. For whoever does these things is detestable to the LORD; and because of these detestable things the LORD your God will drive them out before you. You shall be blameless before the LORD your God. For those nations, which you shall dispossess, listen to those who practice witchcraft and to diviners, but as for you, the LORD your God has not allowed you to do so."*

<u>Joshua 6:18-19</u> *"And you, by all means abstain from the accursed things, lest you become accursed when you take of the accursed things, and make the camp of Israel a curse, and trouble it. But all the silver and gold, and vessels of bronze and iron, are consecrated to the LORD; they shall come into the treasury of the LORD."*

<u>II Chronicles 34</u>
This chapter talks about how Josiah restored the county of Israel to the Lord God. In the same way, we can restore our homes to the sanctifying work of His Spirit.

163

Psalm 12:8 *"The wicked strut about on every side, when vileness is exalted among the sons of men."*

Psalms 101:3 *"I will set no worthless thing before my eyes."*

Isaiah 30:22 *"And you will defile your graven images overlaid with silver, and your molten images plated with gold, You will scatter them as an impure thing, and say to them, 'Be gone!'"*

Acts 15:19-20 *"Therefore I judge that we should not trouble those from among the Gentiles who are turning to God, but that we write to them to abstain from things polluted by idols, from sexual immorality, from things strangled, and from blood."*

Acts 19:11-20 *"God was performing extraordinary miracles by the hands of Paul, so that handkerchiefs or aprons were even carried from his body to the sick, and the diseases left them, and the evil spirits went out. But also some of the Jewish exorcists, who went from place to place, attempted to name over those who had the evil spirits the name of the Lord Jesus, saying, 'I adjure you by Jesus whom Paul preaches.' Seven sons of one Sceva, a Jewish chief priest, were doing this. And the evil spirit answered and said to them, 'I recognize Jesus, and I know about Paul, but who are you?' And the man, in whom was the evil spirit, leaped on them and subdued all of them and overpowered them, so that they fled out of that house naked and wounded. This became known to all, both Jews and Greeks, who lived in Ephesus; and fear fell upon them all and the name of the Lord Jesus was being magnified. Many also of those who had believed kept coming, confessing, and disclosing their practices. And many of those who practiced magic brought their books together and began burning them in the sight of everyone; and they counted up the price of them and found it fifty thousand pieces of silver. So the word of the Lord was growing mightily and prevailing."*

1 Corinthians 10: 6-7 *"Now these things became our examples, to the intent that we should not lust after evil things as they also lusted. And do not become idolaters, as were some of them. As it is*

written, 'The people sat down to eat and drink, and rose up to play.'"

II Corinthians 6:17-18 *"Therefore, Come out from among them and be separate, says the Lord. Do not touch what is unclean, and I will receive you. I will be a Father to you, and you shall be My sons and daughters, says the LORD Almighty."*

1 John 5:21 *"Little children, keep yourselves from idols. Amen."*

WHY WE DO DELIVERANCE

John 8:36 *"For if the Son makes you free, you will be free indeed."*

John 10:10 *"The thief comes only to steal and kill and destroy; I (Jesus) came that they may have life and have it abundantly."*

Ephesians 6:12 *"For our struggle is not against flesh and blood, but against the rulers, against the powers, against the world forces of this darkness, against the spiritual forces of wickedness in the heavenly places."*

Philippians 2:12 *"...Work out your own salvation with fear and trembling."* (Indicates that coming to full freedom in Christ is a process that starts with salvation.)

I John 4:3 *"...And every spirit that does not confess Jesus - is not from God; this is the spirit of the antichrist, of which you have heard that it is coming, and now it is already in the world."*

CHRISTIANS CAN BE DEMONIZED

The following passages of Scripture are some instances of demonization of believers of God (Jews and Christians) from the New Testament after Pentecost:

1. The Canaanite woman was a woman of faith: *"And a Canaanite woman from that region came out and began to cry out, saying, 'Have mercy on me, Lord, Son of David; my*

daughter is cruelly demon-possessed'" But He did not answer her a word. And His disciples came and implored Him, saying, 'Send her away, because she keeps shouting at us.' But He answered and said, 'I was sent only to the lost sheep of the house of Israel.' But she came and began to bow down before Him, saying, 'Lord, help me!' And He answered and said, "It is not good to take the children's bread and throw it to the dogs.' But she said, 'Yes, Lord; but even the dogs feed on the crumbs which fall from their masters' table.' Then Jesus said to her, 'O woman, your faith is great; it shall be done for you as you wish.' And her daughter was healed at once." <u>Matthew 15:22-28</u>

2. <u>Peter</u>: *"Peter took Him aside and began to rebuke Him, saying, 'God forbid it, Lord! This shall never happen to you.' But He turned and said to Peter, 'Get behind Me, Satan! You are a stumbling block to me; for you are not setting your mind on God's interests, but man's.'"* <u>Matthew 16:22-23</u>

3. <u>Man in church</u>: *"Just then there was a man in their synagogue with an unclean spirit; and he cried out..."* <u>Mark 1:23</u>

4. <u>James and John's being told by Jesus</u>: *"You know not what spirit you are of..."* <u>Luke 9:52-56</u>

5. <u>Woman (daughter of Abraham) with spirit of infirmity</u>: *"And, behold, there was a woman which had a spirit of infirmity eighteen years, and was bowed together, and could in no wise lift up herself.... And ought not this woman, being a daughter of Abraham, whom Satan hath bound, lo, these eighteen years, be loosed from this bond on the Sabbath day?"* <u>Luke 13:11, 16</u>

6. <u>Jesus' Disciple Judas</u>: Judas being demonized by Satan <u>John 6:70-71, 13:27</u>

7. <u>Believers</u>: *"And God wrought special miracles by the hands of Paul: So that from his body were brought unto the sick handkerchiefs or aprons, and the diseases departed from them, and the evil spirits went out of them."* <u>Acts 19:11-12</u> (These

people were believers, since the Bible says that it is dangerous to not "fill" the clean, empty house and he would have known it would not be good to just cast out evil spirits in people that did not know the Lord yet.)

CHRISTIANS CAN HAVE UNGODLY SOUL TIES

Mark 10: 6 "*...But from the beginning of creation, God made them male and female. For this reason a man shall leave his father and mother, and the two shall become one flesh; so they are no longer two, but one flesh. "What therefore God has joined together let no man separate.*"

I Corinthians 6:16 "*...Or do you not know that the one who joins himself to a prostitute is one body with her? For he says, "the two shall become one flesh.*"

WHO CAN BE DELIVERED

Proverbs 11:6 "*The righteousness of the upright will deliver them.*"

Joel 2:32 "And *it will come about that whoever calls on the name of the Lord will be delivered.*"

OUR JOB (AS CHRISTIANS)

Exodus 23:30 "*By little and little I will drive them out from before thee, until thou be increased, and inherit the land.*"

Isaiah 58:8 "*Is this not the fast, which I choose, to loosen the bonds of wickedness, to undo the bands of the yoke, and to let the oppressed go free and break every yoke?*"

Isaiah 61:1-3 "*The Spirit of the Lord GOD is upon me; because the LORD hath anointed me to preach good tidings unto the meek; he hath sent me to bind up the brokenhearted, to proclaim liberty to the captives, and the opening of the prison to them that are bound; To proclaim the acceptable year of the LORD, and the day of vengeance of our God; to comfort all that mourn; To appoint unto them that mourn in Zion, to give unto them beauty for ashes, the oil of joy for mourning, the garment of praise for the spirit of heaviness; that they might be called trees of righteousness, the planting of the LORD, that he might be glorified."*

Daniel 11:32 *"The people who know their God will display strength and take action."*

Matthew 8:16-17 *"When the evening was come, they brought unto him many that were possessed with devils: and he cast out the spirits with his word and healed all that were sick: That it might be fulfilled which was spoken by Esaias the prophet, saying, Himself took our infirmities, and bare our sicknesses."*

Matthew 10:7-8 *"And as ye go, preach, saying, the kingdom of heaven is at hand. Heal the sick, cleanse the lepers, raise the dead, and cast out devils: freely ye have received, freely give."*

Mark 1:39 *"And he preached in their synagogues throughout all Galilee and cast out devils."*

Mark 16:17 "And *these signs shall follow them that believe; in my name shall they cast out devils; they shall speak with new tongues..."*

Luke 4:18 *"The Spirit of the Lord is upon me, because he anointed me to preach the gospel to the poor. He has sent me to proclaim release to the captives, and recovery of sight to the blind, to set free those who are oppressed..."*

Luke 7:21 *"And in that same hour he cured many of their infirmities and plagues, and of evil spirits; and unto many that were blind he gave sight."*

Luke 8:2 *"And certain women, who had been healed of evil spirits and infirmities, Mary called Magdalene, out of whom went seven devils..."*

Luke 10:17-19 *"And the seventy returned again with joy, saying, Lord, even the devils are subject unto us through thy name. And he said unto them, I beheld Satan as lightning fall from heaven. Behold, I give unto you power to tread on serpents and scorpions, and over all the power of the enemy: and nothing shall by any means hurt you."*

John 14:12 *"Truly, truly, I say to you, he who believes in me, the works that I do, he will do also; and greater works than these he will do; because I go to the Father."*

Acts 5:16 *"There came also a multitude out of the cities round about unto Jerusalem, bringing sick folks, and them which were vexed with unclean spirits: and they were healed everyone."*

Acts 8:7 *"For unclean spirits, crying with loud voice, came out of many that were possessed with them: and many taken with palsies, and that were lame, were healed."*

Acts 10:38 *"How God anointed Jesus of Nazareth with the Holy Ghost and with power: who went about doing good and healing all that were oppressed of the devil; for God was with him."*

Acts 19:11 *"God was performing extraordinary miracles by the hands of Paul..."* (Paul is no different from you or me. God will use us just as much if we are willing.)

II Corinthians 10:3-5 *"For though we walk in the flesh, we do not war according to the flesh, for the weapons of our warfare are not of the flesh, but divinely powerful for the destruction of fortresses (strongholds). We are destroying speculations and every lofty thing raised up against the knowledge of God, and we are taking every thought captive to the obedience of Christ..."*

Ephesians 2:4-6 *"God...raised us up with Him, and seated us with Him in the heavenly places..."*

Ephesians 6: 10-17 *"Finally, be strong in the Lord and in the strength of His might. Put on the full armor of God, so that you will be able to stand firm against the schemes of the devil. For our struggle is not against flesh and blood, but against the rulers, against the powers, against the world forces of this darkness, against the spiritual forces of wickedness in the heavenly places. Therefore, take up the full armor of God, so that you will be able to resist in the evil day, and having done everything, to stand firm. Stand firm therefore, having girded your loins with truth, and having put on the breastplate of righteousness, and having shod your feet with the preparation of the gospel of peace; in addition to all, taking up the shield of faith with which you will be able to extinguish all the flaming arrows of the evil one. And take the helmet of salvation, and the sword of the Spirit, which is the Word of God. With all prayer and petition pray at all times in the Spirit, and with this in view, be on the alert with all perseverance and petition for all the saints, and pray on my behalf, that utterance may be given to me in the opening of my mouth, to make known with boldness the mystery of the gospel, for which I am an ambassador in chains; that in proclaiming it I may speak boldly, as I ought to speak."*

<u>Philippians 4:4-9</u> *"Rejoice in the Lord always; again I will say, rejoice! Let your gentle spirit be known to all men. The Lord is near. Be anxious for nothing, but in everything by prayer and supplication with thanksgiving let your requests be made known to God. And the peace of God, which surpasses all comprehension, will guard your hearts and your minds in Christ Jesus. Finally, brethren, whatever is true, whatever is honorable, whatever is right, whatever is pure, whatever is lovely, whatever is of good repute, if there is any excellence and if anything worthy of praise, dwell on these things. The things you have learned and received and heard and seen in me, practice these things, and the God of peace will be with you."*

<u>WHAT DELIVERANCE DOES FOR US</u>

<u>Ezekiel 36:26</u> *"Moreover, I will give you a new heart and put a new spirit within you; and I will remove the heart of stone from your flesh and give you a heart of flesh."*

1 Timothy 4:1 *"But the Spirit explicitly says that in later times some will fall away from the faith, paying attention to deceitful spirits and doctrines of demons…"*

We need deliverance!

MISCELLANEOUS DELIVERANCE VERSES

Matthew 12:43-45 *"Now when the unclean spirit goes out of a man, it passes through waterless places seeking rest, and does not find it. Then it says, 'I will return to my house from which I came"; and when it comes, it finds it unoccupied, swept, and put in order. Then it goes and takes along with it seven other spirits more wicked than itself, and they go in and live there; and the last state of that man becomes worse than the first. That is the way it will also be with this evil generation."* (Note: Our "houses" need to be cleansed and put in order but FILLED with the Holy Spirit of God. This is why we do not do deliverance on non-Christians.)

APPENDIX: DELIVERANCE WORKSHEET WITH EXPLANATIONS INCLUDED

Start by using this worksheet with helpful explanations. Later once you fully understand the process, you can just use the basic worksheet.

Permission is granted to make copies of this worksheet.

Let's Get Started

- In the early stages of deliverance, it will be important to set aside chunks of time to devote to the work you will be doing. An hour minimum is recommended.
- Remove all distractions.
- Start with the prayer to set yourself up in the spiritual realm.
- As you know come before the Lord, turn off your mind from being focused on distractions, and ask the Holy Spirit to reveal a root stronghold. (At this point, He may reveal more than one. You can write these all down before proceeding with the below.)
- Once you have identified the stronghold or strongholds He wants to work with you on that day, start the below process.

1. **Describe the memory you are having as if you were outside looking in at it.** (Note: You can think about this, you can verbalize it out loud to yourself or another, or you can write about it. It is up to you.)_____
   _____
   _____
   _____

2. Now **describe the memory as it <u>felt</u> at the time you had it**. (Note: Dig deep into your memory and the emotions you had at that time and finish the sentence below. **When that happened to me, I felt:** _____
   _____
   _____
   _____

a. Note: As you remember how this memory felt at the time, there is a good chance you will cry – even if you did not cry at the time it actually happened. It is very important that you allow yourself to grieve. Do not hold anything back. And do not cut yourself short from taking time to grieve. What you will find is not self-pity but true deep pain that was somehow stuffed deep down inside of you and you (or someone else) did not allow you to express it at the time. Often, if you were a child, you did not know how to express it because you did not understand what it was that really happened. But now, let it all out! Because in so doing, healing will take place and many times demons are also released through our tears.

3. **Ask the Lord to break the stronghold.** "Father God, in Jesus' name, I ask that You take back the ground that was given to the enemy when_____ _____, and break the stronghold from my soul." (See section on Strongholds for more info as needed.)

4. **Ask the Lord to cancel any word curses or spells that were spoken over or to you at that time.** "Father God, in Jesus' name, I ask that You cancel the word curses and/or spells that were spoken over me." (Note: Be as specific as you remember. If you do not remember, He does. And this prayer will take care of even those things.) (See Section on Curses and Spells for more info as needed.)

5. **Identify the generational iniquities in the event:**_____
_____
_____
_____
_____

a. Now **repent for those generational iniquities** and ask the Lord to severe their cords from you. (See section on Generational Iniquities for more info as needed.)

6. **Identify and repent for any sins <u>you</u> committed during or through the years after this event.** (Note: Did you sin in any way during this memory or since it occurred? Most likely you did. Take time repent for your sin and ask for God's forgiveness. It is never right to sin over someone else's sin. So we must be humble and confess and repent for our sin in these matters.)_____

_____
_____
_____

7. **List the names of those involved who hurt and offended you.**_____

_____
_____
_____

    a. **Pray the prayer to forgive each one individually.** (See Prayer to Grant Forgiveness.)

    b. Then **ask the Lord** on an individual basis:
        i. **To break the soul ties** with each off these people. (See section on soul ties.)
        ii. **To lead each of them to repentance and salvation**
        iii. **To take them into His hands as you release complete and total control** of them to Him, for Him to work with them.

    c. Then **ask Him if you need to go to anyone to ask for forgiveness** for any part you had in the matter.

8. Now **renounce all spirits of the enemy** that come to mind as being involved. If you felt rejection, then spirit of rejection. If you felt fear, then spirit of fear. Etc. (See section on demons.)

9. Once you have renounced, **command all spirits to leave you now** and go to Jesus to be dealt with.

10. **Ask Jesus to cleanse you and heal you with the blood of Jesus**.

11. **Ask Jesus to call all pieces of your soul** that split off with the trauma back to His hands. Ask Him to cleanse them, heal them, integrate them back into your soul, and bring them to your current age of today.

12. **Ask the Lord to give you a fresh filling of His Holy Spirit** in all places vacated by the enemy.

APPENDIX: DELIVERANCE WORKSHEET (BASIC FORMAT)

Once you have a good grasp of the steps to be taken to gain freedom, you can use this shortened version of recording your strongholds, as they are then broken.

Permission is granted to make copies of this worksheet.

Let's Get Started

1. **Describe the memory you are having as if you were outside looking in at it.**

2. Now **describe the memory as it <u>felt</u> at the time you had it. When that happened to me, I felt:**

3. **Ask the Lord to break the stronghold.**

4. **Ask the Lord to cancel any word curses or spells that were spoken over or to you at that time.**

5. **Identify the generational iniquities in the event, repent for them, and ask the Lord to sever their cords from you.**

6. Identify and repent for any sins <u>you</u> committed during or through the years after this event.

7. **List the names of those involved who hurt and offended you.** (Pray to forgive each one individually, ask the Lord to break the soul ties and lead them to repentance, and then release them to Him.)

8. **Renounce all spirits of the enemy** that come to mind as being involved in your stronghold.

9. **Command all spirits to leave** you now and go to Jesus to be dealt with.

10. **Ask Jesus to cleanse you and heal you with the blood of Jesus and to call all pieces of your soul back to His hands**, cleansing them, healing them, integrating them back into your soul, and bringing them to your current age of today.

11. **Ask the Lord to give you a fresh filling of His Holy Spirit in all places vacated by the enemy**.

Appendix: <u>POCKET QUICK-AIDE CARDS</u>
You can print out & cut these cards up, to keep them handy.

PRAYER TO BREAK STRONGHOLDS	DAILY PRAYER FOR UNSAVED
Father, in Jesus name, I ask that You take back the ground that was given to the enemy when (Incident), and I ask that You break that stronghold from my soul. I renounce all lies of the enemy and ask that you would cleanse and heal me with the blood of Jesus.	Father, in Jesus name, *I ask that You bind the enemy from (Name); take off all the veils of the enemy; & open his eyes, ears, heart, and soul to the truth of God. I also ask that You bring someone to him who can lead him to salvation.*
PRAYER TO FORGIVE	**STEPS TO FORGIVENESS**
As an act of my will, I choose to forgive (Name of Person) and I ask that You give me Your Grace to do so, from the bottom of my heart. (See "Steps to Forgiveness" card.)	*Take 24 hours max to process. Then… *Cease thinking about it! *Pray the Prayer to Forgive. *Give it to God and let go! *Do not allow yourself to think about it from the 24-hour mark going forward.
DAILY PRAYER FOR GRACE & ISOLATION	**OVERCOMING ANXIETY**
Father, in Jesus name, I ask that You give me Your Grace to overcome every ungodly situation I will face today. (Grace is God working through you to give you His desire & His power to do His will.) I also ask that You put me in complete isolation from the enemy today, so that nothing I say or do can be perceived.	*Be anxious for nothing, but in everything by prayer and supplication with thanksgiving let your requests be made known to God. And the peace of God, which surpasses all understanding, will guard your hearts and your minds in Christ Jesus.* <u>Philippians 4:6-7</u>

Appendix: <u>PRAYER FOR UNSAVED LOVED ONES</u>

"And even if our gospel is veiled, it is veiled to those who are perishing, on whose case the god of this world has blinded the minds of the unbelieving so that they might not see the light of the gospel of the glory of Christ, who is the image of God."
<u>II Corinthians 4:3-4</u>

The following is also a good prayer for the carnal Christian or even ourselves in times of confusion.

Father, in Jesus' name, I ask that You bind the enemy from (Name of Person); **take off all the veils of the enemy; and open his eyes, ears, heart, and soul to the truth of God. I also ask that You bring someone to him who can lead him to salvation.**

<u>Note 1</u>: When your loved one starts coming around, DO NOT STOP PRAYING THIS PRAYER. Keep praying through until he receives salvation and has gone through a deliverance process.

<u>Note 2</u>: This is also a good prayer to pray for loved ones who are believers but are having a hard time getting on the right road.

<u>Note 3</u>: Pray this prayer over yourself as well, especially in times when you are feeling confused. You will be amazed at how quickly the Lord shows you His truth in the situation. We are so quick to buy into the lies of the enemy! This is why this prayer is an essential tool for us to use frequently.

Appendix: <u>SALVATION IN THREE PARTS</u>

<u>Recommended Prayer Prior To Studying The Below</u>
Father, bind the enemy from me and open my eyes
to the truth of God, that I may truly know You
and serve You with Excellence.

<u>THE FULLNESS OF SALVATION AS GOD INTENDED</u>

- *Repentance for forgiveness of sin*
- *Baptism in water to die to sin & come alive in Christ*
- *Baptism in Holy Spirit to be empowered by God*

Get out your Bible and take the time to read and really understand what the scriptures say, so that you can then explain it to others in a way that will help them understand too. There is much faulty teaching in the church about salvation, baptism with water, and baptism with the Holy Spirit and we need to be able to correct the teaching, so that every Son/Daughter of God can receive the fullness of what He has for every follower of Jesus Christ.

<u>REPENTANCE TO GOD FOR FORGIVENESS OF SIN</u>

- *Everyone has sinned.*
  - <u>Romans 3:23</u> *...for ALL have sinned and fall short of the glory of God.*
- *When we sin, we become a slave to sin.*
  - <u>Romans 6:6</u> *tells us about being slaves of sin. (Passage below.)*
- *Repentance has to be from the heart, not the head. You must feel conviction for your wrongdoings.*
- *Repentance is a decision to do a 180-degree turn away from sin.*

<u>BAPTISM IN WATER TO DIE TO SIN &</u>
<u>COME ALIVE IN CHRIST</u>
What is Baptism? Generally speaking, the church over the many years has reduced baptism to simply being symbolic of the death,

burial, and resurrection of Jesus. However, when we begin to look at it as also very literal (according to Scripture) – in that we die with Christ (as we submerge) and come up alive in Christ and are made new! (as we arise from the water) - then we begin to realize that baptism in water is extremely important in and of itself, and that it is an essential step to full true salvation!

- Romans 6:3-14 *"Or do you not know that <u>all of us who have been baptized into Christ Jesus have been baptized into His death?</u> 4 Therefore <u>we have been buried with Him through baptism into death, so that as Christ was raised from the dead through the glory of the Father, so we too might walk in newness of life.</u> 5 For if we have become united with Him in the likeness of His death, certainly we shall also be in the likeness of His resurrection, 6 knowing this, that <u>our old self was crucified with Him, in order that our body of sin might be done away with, so that we would no longer be slaves to sin;</u> 7 for <u>he who has died is freed from sin.</u> 8 Now <u>if we have died with Christ, we believe that we shall also live with Him,</u> 9 knowing that Christ, having been raised from the dead, is never to die again; death no longer is master over Him. 10 <u>For the death that He died, He died to sin once for all; but the life that He lives, He lives to God.</u> 11 Even so consider yourselves to be dead to sin, but alive to God in Christ Jesus. 12 Therefore do not let sin reign in your mortal body so that you obey its lusts, 13 and do not go on presenting the members of your body to sin as instruments of unrighteousness; but present yourselves to God as those alive from the dead, and your members as instruments of righteousness to God. 14 For sin shall not be master over you, for you are not under law but under grace."*

- **<u>Water baptism is an act of obedience.</u>**
  - *<u>We are to follow Jesus' example.</u> John baptized Jesus as our example. He did a baptism of repentance and water at one time. For us, we start with repenting of our sins and then receiving Christ as our Lord and Savior. As soon as possible after*

181

that *(ideally the same day), we follow with water baptism.*

- ***Baptism with water is meant to be literally dying to sin and rising up again in Jesus Christ*** *– or dying to the old man and raising up in the new man! We are, literally, a new creature! When Jesus died on the cross, OUR OLD MAN was executed and died with Christ.*
  - Colossians 2:12 *Therefore we have been buried with Him through baptism into death, so that as Christ was raised from the dead through the glory of the Father, so we too might walk in newness of life.*

Who should be baptized?

- *Everyone who has repented for his sins and is seeking after God with his entire heart – with the intent to follow Him and obey Him in everything that He asks. Those who have entered a Father-child relationship with God the Father – made possible by the death of Jesus Christ who died to pay for our sins.*

Can an infant be baptized?

- *Because repentance and relationship are a part of baptism, then an infant cannot be baptized for the purpose of salvation. He can, however, be "dedicated" to God.*

Can we be sprinkled to be baptized?

- *In the New Testament, the Greek word for baptize is baptizó and it means: to dip, sink, submerge.*

Can anyone do the baptizing?

- *Any True Child of God can baptize a new believer. See what is often called The Great Commission. These were Jesus' last words while on earth as He gave instruction to the Apostles for all True Believers in Christ going forward through time.*

- o Matthew 28:16-20 *¹⁶But the eleven disciples proceeded to Galilee, to the mountain, which Jesus had designated. ¹⁷When they saw Him, they worshiped Him; but some were doubtful. ¹⁸And Jesus came up and spoke to them, saying, "All authority has been given to Me in heaven and on earth. ¹⁹__Go__ therefore and __make disciples__ of all the nations, __baptizing__ them in the name of the Father and the Son and the Holy Spirit, ²⁰__teaching__ them to observe all that I commanded you; and lo, I am with you always, even to the end of the age."*

Is water baptism necessary for true salvation? In other words, do we have to be baptized to be saved?

- *Many will say no. However, there is are scriptures that make it quite clear, that this may not be the case, especially when there is no reason for the person not to be water baptized.*
- *Every time there was repentance in Acts there was ALWAYS baptism.*
- *Most churches teach salvation is only by faith. But faith includes steps of action (works). Following are some scriptures that combine water baptism and salvation.*
    - o *From The Great Commission in* Mark 16:15-18 *And He said to them, "__Go__ into all the world and __preach__ the gospel to every creature. __He who believes and is baptized will be saved__; but he who does not believe will be condemned. And these __signs__ will follow those who believe: In My name they will __cast out demons__; they will __speak with new tongues__; they will take up serpents; and if they drink anything deadly, it will by __no means hurt them__; they will __lay hands on the sick__, and they will recover."*

    - o John 3:5 *Jesus answered, "Truly, truly, I say to you, unless one is born of water and the Spirit he cannot enter into the kingdom of God."*

- I Peter 3:18-22 *(Peter) 18 For Christ also died for sins once for all, the just for the unjust, so that He might bring us to God, having been put to death in the flesh, but made alive in the spirit; 19 in which also He went and made proclamation to the spirits now in prison, 20 who once were disobedient, when the patience of God kept waiting in the days of Noah, during the construction of the ark, in which a few, that is, eight persons, were brought safely through the water. 21 Corresponding to that, <u>baptism now saves you</u>—not the removal of dirt from the flesh, but an appeal to God for a good conscience—through the resurrection of Jesus Christ, 22 who is at the right hand of God, having gone into heaven, after angels and authorities and powers had been subjected to Him.*

- Acts 2:36-47 *Therefore let all the house of Israel know for certain that God has made Him both Lord and Christ—this Jesus whom you crucified." Now when they heard this, they were pierced to the heart, and said to Peter and the rest of the apostles, "Brethren, what shall we do?" 38 Peter said to them, "<u>Repent, and each of you be baptized in the name of Jesus Christ for the forgiveness of your sins; and you will receive the gift of the Holy Spirit</u>. 39 "For the promise is for you and your children and for all who are far off, as many as the Lord our God will call to Himself." 40 And with many other words he solemnly testified and kept on exhorting them, saying, "Be saved from this perverse generation!" 41 So then, those who had received his word were baptized; and that day there were added about three thousand souls. 42 They were continually devoting themselves to the apostles' teaching and to fellowship, to the breaking of bread and to prayer. 43 Everyone kept feeling a sense of awe; and many wonders and signs were taking place through the apostles. 44 And all those* *who had believed were together and had all things in common; 45 and they began selling their property and possessions and were sharing them with all, as anyone might have need. 46 Day by day continuing with one mind in the temple, and breaking bread from house to house, they were taking their meals together with gladness and sincerity of heart, 47 praising God and having favor with all the people. And the Lord was adding to their number day by day those who were being saved.*

o **What about the thief on the cross?** *There is one clear exception in scripture and that is the thief on the cross who said yes to Christ. Obviously baptism was not something he could do at that point – and he did obviously go to Heaven. But do we make a doctrine out of the one exception, or do we go by the many other examples in the New Testament where baptism with water and the Holy Spirit were done soon after, if not immediately after, repentance for salvation?*

o **Bottom line:** *Why take the chance? Get baptized as soon as you can after you become a Child of God.*

MATTHEW 3
WE ARE TO FOLLOW JESUS' EXAMPLE: 3 STEPS

Now in those days John the Baptist came, preaching in the wilderness of Judea, saying, "Repent, for the kingdom of heaven is at hand. For this is the one referred to by Isaiah the prophet when he said, 'The voice of one crying in the wilderness, make ready the way of the Lord, make His paths straight!'" Now John himself had a garment of camel's hair and a leather belt around his waist; and his food was locusts and wild honey. Then Jerusalem was going out to him, and all Judea and the entire district around the Jordan: and he was baptizing them in the Jordan River, as they confessed their sins. But when he saw many of the Pharisees and Sadducees *coming for baptism, he said to them, "You brood of vipers, who warned you to flee from the wrath to come? Therefore bear fruit in keeping with repentance; and do not suppose that you can say to yourselves, 'We have Abraham for our father'; for I say to you that from these stones God is able to raise up children to Abraham. The axe is already laid at the root of the trees; therefore every tree that does not bear good fruit is cut down and thrown into the fire. As for me, I baptize you with water for repentance, but He who is coming after me is mightier than I, and I am not fit to remove His sandals; He will baptize you with the Holy Spirit and fire. His winnowing fork is in His hand, and He will thoroughly clear His threshing floor; and He will gather His wheat into the barn, but He will burn up the chaff with unquenchable fire." ¹³ Then Jesus arrived from Galilee at the Jordan coming to John, to be baptized by him. ¹⁴ But John tried to prevent Him, saying, "I have need to be baptized by You, and do You come to me?" ¹⁵ But Jesus answering said to him, "Permit it at this time; for in this way it is fitting for us to fulfill all righteousness." Then he permitted Him. ¹⁶ After being baptized, Jesus came up immediately from the water; and behold, the heavens were opened, and he saw the Spirit of God descending as a dove and lighting on Him, ¹⁷ and behold, a voice out of the heavens said, "This is My beloved Son, in whom I am well-pleased." (Salvation, Water Baptism, Holy Spirit Baptism)*

BAPTISM IN HOLY SPIRIT TO BE EMPOWERED BY GOD
All references are from the New American Standard Bible, unless otherwise specified.

When was the Holy Spirit given to mankind?
* John 20: 19-23 *So when it was evening on that day, the first day of the week, and when the doors were shut where the disciples were, for fear of the Jews, Jesus came and stood in their midst and said to them, "Peace be with you." And when He had said this, He showed them both His hands and His side. The disciples then rejoiced when they saw the Lord. So Jesus said to them again, "Peace be with you; as the Father has sent Me, I also send you." And when He had said this, He breathed on them and said to them,*

"Receive the Holy Spirit. "If you forgive the sins of any, their sins have been forgiven them; if you retain the sins of any, they have been retained."

The coming of the Holy Spirit upon people always followed repentance for salvation and preceded ministry and life in the church as a believer. Baptism of the Holy Spirit is how we receive power.

- Jesus *did not start His earthly ministry until he had been baptized with water, immediately followed by the Holy Spirit descending upon Him as a dove.*

- *The First Church in Acts Jesus did not allow the start of the church until after they had been baptized with the Holy Spirit.*
    - Luke 24:48 *And behold, I am sending forth the promise of My Father upon you; but you are to stay in the city until you are clothed with power from on high.*
    - Acts 1:4-8 *Gathering them together, He commanded them not to leave Jerusalem, but to wait for what the Father had promised, "Which," He said, "you heard of from Me; 5 for John baptized with water, but you will be baptized with the Holy Spirit not many days from now." 6 So when they had come together, they were asking Him, saying, "Lord, is it at this time You are restoring the kingdom to Israel?" 7 He said to them, "It is not for you to know times or epochs which the Father has fixed by His own authority; 8 but you will receive power when the Holy Spirit has come upon you; and you shall be My witnesses both in Jerusalem, and in all Judea and Samaria, and even to the remotest part of the earth."*

The Day of Pentecost
- Acts 2:1-4 *When the day of Pentecost had come, they were all together in one place. And suddenly there came from*

heaven a noise like a violent rushing wind, and it filled the whole house where they were sitting. And there appeared to them tongues as of fire distributing themselves, and they rested on each one of them. And they were all filled with the Holy Spirit and began to speak with other tongues, as the Spirit was giving them utterance.

Do we have to be Holy Spirit baptized to be saved? Don't we receive the Holy Spirit at Salvation?

- *We do not receive the Holy Spirit at Salvation until we have been baptized in the Holy Spirit. Acts 8:12-17 And when they believed Philip preaching the good news about the kingdom of God and the name of Jesus Christ, they were being baptized, men and women alike. Even Simon himself believed; and after being baptized, he continued on with Philip, and as he observed signs and great miracles taking place, he was constantly amazed. Now when the apostles in Jerusalem heard that Samaria had received the word of God, they sent them Peter and John, who came down and prayed for them that they might receive the Holy Spirit.* **For He had not yet fallen upon any of them; they had simply been baptized in the name of the Lord Jesus.** *Then they began laying their hands on them, and they were receiving the Holy Spirit.*

Do I have to speak in tongues after Baptism of the Holy Spirit?

We often meet those in the church who will try to refute tongues (prayer language) as being for every Christian. The answer is simple and irrefutable:

- *It is part of The Great Commission in Mark which was given to the Apostles to carry forward in teaching and written form to all believers of all times.*
  - *Mark 16:15-18 Jesus said: "And these signs will accompany those who believe: In my name they will drive out demons; they will speak in new tongues; ... they will place their hands on sick people, and they will get well."*
- *This is for every believer and we are not to forbid it.*

- o <u>I Corinthians 14:5, 39</u> *I would like every one of you to speak in tongues... Therefore, my brothers, be eager to prophecy, and do not forbid speaking in tongues.*
- *EVERY TIME tongues are spoken about following Holy Spirit baptism, the Bible says, "<u>All</u> spoke in tongues."*
- *Other scriptural references to tongues NOT connected with the baptism by Holy Spirit are probably referring to the GIFT of tongues, which is different from tongues as a prayer language.*

What does it look like to be full of the Holy Spirit?
- *We see multiple times the disciples were "FULL" of the Holy Spirit & how they spoke with confidence and boldness.*
  - o *For example in <u>Acts 4:13</u> Peter and John preached to the rulers and elders with great boldness and without hindrance: "<u>Now as they (the rulers and elders) observed the confidence of Peter and John</u> and understood that they were uneducated and untrained men, they were amazed, and began to recognize them as having been with Jesus."*
  - o *In <u>Acts 4:31</u> as the disciples were meeting it says, "And when they had prayed, the place where they had gathered together was shaken, and <u>they were all filled with the Holy Spirit and began to speak the word of God with boldness</u>."*
- *The disciples had Godly wisdom and understanding beyond what the elders and scribes of that time had.*
- *They walked in authority over darkness - casting out demons, healing the sick, other miracles, signs and wonders.*
- *In <u>Acts 5:17</u> it says that the religious people were filled with jealousy when they saw everything the disciples were doing.*
- *Their faith was action oriented not just talk. Faith without works is dead!*

- *The Holy Spirit also gave the disciples the grace to withstand a lot of persecution. Many, if not all, of the disciples were martyred for their faiths*

The Book of Acts is the real Christian life.

- *We have been blinded and deceived by the traditions of men and false doctrines in the church. We need to return to the Word of God and read it as it is and believe it for what it says. God has promised us an abundant life more than anything we could ever plan for ourselves. Abide in Him and walk the narrow path, which leads to life.*

Can the devil hear our tongues?

- People use this verse: <u>I Corinthians 14:2</u> *For one who speaks in a tongue does not speak to men but to God; for no one understands, but in his spirit he speaks mysteries.*

  - *This verse is very weak support for the possibility that Satan cannot hear tongues. He is spirit and if we are speaking in the spirit, he would be able to hear and understand. In fact, he can also speak to us mind-to-mind. And because of this, he can tell what we are thinking.*

  - *The bottom line is: Who cares if he can or can't? It doesn't change the power of the communication between God and us.*

MINISTERING THE BAPTISM WITH THE HOLY SPIRIT

PRAY: *As soon as possible after you have accepted Jesus as Lord and Savior, ask the Father for the baptism with the Holy Spirit.*

RECEIVE: *Lift your hands in a prayerful attitude as someone who is baptized with the Holy Spirit lays hands on you. Receive by faith. Expect to speak in tongues.*

SPEAK: *Although the gift of tongues is supernatural, you still have to speak. As hands are laid upon you, the Holy Spirit will put strange sounds in your mind. Start mouthing these sounds. At first it may sound like babble or groanings, but as you continue the words and sentences will become more distinct. Some people receive only a few words or sentences, while others gush forth in a more complete language. Be thankful for what the Holy Spirit has given you and use it often. As you use your prayer language, new words often come. The gift of tongues comes supernaturally; the everyday use of your prayer language is natural. This means that you can speak in tongues at will, wherever you desire to pray in tongues. The more you use your prayer language; you will gain confidence and boldness in your prayer life.*

> **Note**: *Some of us have been taught that tongues are "not for today" or even in some cases that "tongues are demonic." This is clearly not the case as we have seen in Scriptures, but sometimes having been taught this will create a mental block in receiving your prayer language. This does NOT mean you were not baptized in the Holy Spirit, but rather that you just need to keep pressing into receiving the prayer language that will eventually come. For me personally, it took many years and even then I had to learn to bypass my mind to receive my prayer language. All to say, do not be discouraged if you are not able to pray in tongues immediately. But at the same time, don't give up until you do!*

Generally speaking, the church over the many years has reduced baptism to simply symbolic of the death, burial, and resurrection of Jesus. However, when we begin to look at it as also very literal (according to Scripture) – in that we die with Christ (as we submerge) and come up alive in Christ and made new! – then we begin to realize that baptism in water is extremely important in and of itself, and that it is an essential step to full true salvation!

Testimony 1: *This week has been filled with highs and lows since my re-baptism. On Sunday, I felt new levels of freedom and it was easier for me to focus on the Lord. I felt really content. I had great clarity of mind and kept declaring God's love for me and His hand in my life. I was cleaning out my room and found old prayers and journals about ex-boyfriends. I couldn't relate to my past struggles - like I am a different person. It was a great feeling to see how the Lord has grown me!*

Testimony 2: *Every day has been so incredible. It's like I have a new boldness. It's exactly what we were talking about in Acts! I feel lighter...cleaner!*

Testimony 3: *I'm feeling great. Definitely being attacked, but I'm able to push through it so much easier now after having been baptized.*

Testimony 4: *After reading and praying through the book of Acts, specifically chapter 2, I knew I needed to be baptized. I had already been previously baptized, but after living through a season of sin and uncleanliness, getting baptized again only seemed right. Especially knowing how crucial it was to the apostles as well as specific words Jesus spoke. The night I was going to get re-baptized I knew Satan did not want me to. I felt so uneasy and almost jumpy on the inside. It was like every demon that I was held captive by knew their time was up. An amazing team of leadership baptized me and guided me through dying with Christ and coming alive in Christ. When I came up from the water I immediately started manifesting. Over the course of several minutes many demons had left me. After a period of time (even though sense of time was absent to me at this point) I was also baptized in the Holy*

Spirit. I had previously been baptized in the Holy Spirit in my life but having been prayed over again was powerful. God knew I needed to be "re-charged." I felt so alive when I got out of the water. I was walking around in wet clothes and I did not care! I fellowshipped until the late hours of the night, and when the night was wrapping up I felt too energized to go home. I drove through the city singing worship music in my car and worshipping from the bottom of my heart! I was also praying for different places as God led me. Many places throughout the city received prayer that night! I know what Jesus did was AMAZING and SO REAL. Walking out my new life with Him has truly been the best thing that has ever happened to me.

WHAT NOW?

- It is also important that you be discipled by someone who loves and knows God the Father, Jesus, and the Holy Spirit. Perhaps the person who baptized you can disciple you or refer you to someone else he trusts to do that with you. Being discipled is extremely important. It will help you to learn more about your new relationship with Jesus and will also help your intimate growth with Him.

- Read the Word of God (Bible) daily so that you learn for yourself what it says. (Start with the New Testament and read from the beginning to the end.)

- Pray anytime and anywhere! God loves it when you talk to Him.

- The sign that true salvation has taken place is that there is a change in you and you are bearing fruit.
  - Matthew 7:18-20 *"Jesus said, 'A good tree cannot produce bad fruit, nor can a bad tree produce good fruit. Every tree that does not bear good fruit is cut down and thrown into the fire. So then, you will know them by their fruits.'"* (Note: This does not mean gifts.)
  - Galatians 5:22-23 *"...the fruit of the Spirit is love, joy, peace, patience, kindness, goodness, faithfulness, gentleness, self-control; against such things there is no law."*

- Go through the deliverance process using this book and one or two trusted and mature Christian friends/mentors who are willing to walk through the process with you and help you. Deeper levels of repentance will be part of the deliverance process as the Holy Spirit reveals.

THE DAY OF MY SALVATION IN JESUS CHRIST

On this date of _____ I _____ repented of my sins before the One and Only True God, creator of all things.

Date and Place I was Water Baptized:_____

Date and Place I was Holy Spirit Baptized:_____

Date and Place I got my tongues prayer language:_____

Take a moment to journal what your thoughts and feelings and other experiences were before, during and after you participated in the above experiences. (This will be an encouragement to you in the future, especially if the enemy tries to tell you that none of it was real.) _____
_____
_____
_____

Based on <u>II Corinthians 5:17</u>, *I claim and declare that I am in Christ Jesus and I am a new creature! The old things have passed away and behold new things have come!*

Special People Who Took Part in Any of the Above With me:_____
_____

Names and Phone Numbers of Those Committed to Helping Me In My New Walk In Christ:_____
_____

Church Recommendations: *(It is important to find a church that teaches about the entire Bible and leaves nothing out. A small sized church is best so that you get to know other fellow believers who can "do life" with you.)*_____
_____
_____

Appendix: <u>SPIRITUAL COVERINGS</u>

When we speak about coverings, let us consider this verse:

"But I would have you know, that the head of every man is Christ; and the head of the woman is the man; and the head of Christ is God."
<u>I Corinthians 11:3</u>

According to this verse, here is the order:
God
Jesus
Man
Woman
(Children)
(Pets ☺)

For a man, his covering is Jesus Christ. For a woman, her covering is man. This does not mean that women do not have direct access to our Father through Jesus, but He has aligned the family structure in a certain way, so that there is order to the authority within that family.

Therefore, every woman is to have the covering of a man. And God has built this into our families. If you are a single woman, your father is your covering. If you are married, your husband is your primary covering but your father is also still an extra layer of protective covering over you as well.

You can have additional coverings such as the pastor at your church, the leader of your Bible study, your boss at work, the government, etc. But remember that your primary coverings are and always will be – your father and/or your husband.

FREQUENTLY ASKED QUESTIONS

My husband is not a believer, so how can he be my covering?
God's word is God's word and His ways are not conditional. It is
very sad that your husband is not a believer, but we do know from
I Corinthians 7:14 that the believing wife sanctifies the unbelieving
husband (and vice versa). Therefore, when you honor your
husband as your covering (regardless of what he is like as a father
or husband), you show him first of all the respect that is of utmost
importance to him. Ephesians 5:33 "*...and the wife must see to it
that she respects her husband.*" You also bring yourself into the
correct alignment as God intended. And as you continue to serve
your husband with actions of love and respect, God and Jesus now
have full access to your husband to work on his heart, to bring him
to a place of repentance. (Women, please remember that you are
NOT the Holy Spirit to your husband and you are to be sure that
you are not getting in God's way of what He is trying to do in and
through your husband to bring him to repentance.)

My father is not a believer, so how can he be my covering? The
answer to this is basically the same as above. When you bring
yourself into the correct alignment within the family (and you must
do this whether or not your mother has shown or is showing your
father that respect herself), then God can begin first of all to
correct the mother. And after He has corrected the mother, He will
then have full access to the father for his correction. (If you are the
"child" of the family, encourage your mother to come into
alignment as God intends. Many families are in deep, deep trouble
or even fragmented through divorce, and most of the times the man
is the one who is blamed. But the truth of the matter is that most of
the time, the woman is out of God's alignment for the family.
Women, I strongly encourage you to pray about this and ask God
for His wisdom and His grace to get you into the correct alignment
within the family, so that He can bring correction to the
husband/father of the home and eventually use your family in
mighty and powerful ways!

**My father is dead, and I am not married. Who should be my
covering?** Pray about this and ask the Lord. Ideally if you have a

brother, uncle, or other relative that you are close to, you could ask him to be your covering. The Bible does say that a neighbor who is near is better than a brother far away (Proverbs 27:10), so if you do not have any close relatives, then you can consider asking your pastor and his wife to be your covering.

- Note: A woman must be careful not to put herself in situations with someone who should not be her covering.
- Note: If your pastor does not know your name and/or does not have contact with you on a regular basis, then you would do best to look for another covering.

What are our responsibilities to our coverings?

(Note: This is extremely important. God can use us in powerful ways to help our coverings.)

- Love our Coverings.
- Pray for our Coverings.
- Support our Coverings.
- Encourage our Coverings.
- Endure with our Coverings.
- Do not complain about our Coverings.
- If you feel your Covering is making a bad choice, APPEAL to him with love, reasoning, and a Godly attitude.
- Ban from your life any TV or movies that make dads look like the idiots of the family (even in jest).

Testimony from 25-year-old Married Woman *I have been married a little over a year and my husband and I have had great difficulties in our marriage. He is not a believer, but he is my covering nevertheless. My father is also not a believer, but I had never seen him as a covering over me. My mother never showed him respect and therefore, neither did I...or at least not like God would have wanted me to. So, I went to my father and first asked his forgiveness for not respecting him. And then I explained to him what the Bible says about coverings. And then I asked him if he would be my secondary covering (my first being my husband). My father wept.*

Testimony from 13-Year-Old Girl *My father and I had not* *spoken for over a year because he was angry with me and punished me by not speaking to me and not allowing me to visit him. Even though what I did seemed very, very small compared to the way he had treated me, I humbled myself and asked his forgiveness for not respecting him and his rules. After I did that, he told me that he wanted to restore our relationship and now we are even going to counseling together to work out our problems. (My father is not a Christian.)*

Testimony from 23-Year-Old Single Woman *I have been estranged from my father for many years. He was an adulterer and child molester, molesting even me when I was very young. In recent years, he has become involved in sex slavery – making frequent visits to Thailand. Nonetheless, I recently asked him if he would be my covering as the Bible states that he is. He said that he was very honored, and he immediately pulled out the Bible and started looking up scriptures. Soon after that, the Lord gave me a vision of the abuse my father had been through himself and then He showed me my father on his knees repenting before God.*

Testimony from 27-Year-Old Single Woman *We had talked to the group about putting the fathers and husbands back where they belong – as heads of the family...as coverings over the family. This young woman had told us that her father had never been part of her life and she wouldn't even know how to get ahold of him. (He lives in Mexico.) We recommended she pray about it and that if the Lord wanted her to do it, He would make a way. Within 5 days of this conversation and prayer, her father texted her out of the clear blue to see how she was doing! (She had not heard from him for years!) Through this, the Lord confirmed to her the position He wanted her father to have over her as her covering.*

Appendix: <u>TELL ME MORE ABOUT CHRISTIANITY</u>

There is one main difference between true Christianity – and all other religions, including Counterfeit Christianity. All other religions rely on GOOD WORKS for salvation and entrance into Heaven. Whereas a TRUE follower of Jesus Christ knows that salvation comes only by God's grace – through faith. It is not something we can earn by good works. It is a gift from God.

"For it is by grace you have been saved, through faith, and that not of yourselves, it is the gift of God; not as a result of works, so that no one may boast." <u>Ephesians 2:8-9</u>

For most people, this sounds too easy to be true. But in some ways it is even harder than thinking you can get to Heaven by doing good works. Because faith requires that we believe what the Word of God, the Bible, says about salvation.

Sad to say, there are even groups who put themselves in the Christian category who are not truly Christians at all. Because they believe they can earn their way to Heaven by good works.

<u>WHAT DOES THE BIBLE SAY ABOUT THIS?</u>

- God says that every one of us has sinned – and sin separates us from God. (Even if you think you are a good person, you still have sinned. For example: Have you ever told a lie? Have you ever stolen anything? Have you ever been involved in sexual sin?)
  - *"For all have sinned and fall short of the glory of God."* <u>Romans 3:23</u>

- Our sin causes a separation between God and us.
  - *"But your iniquities have made a separation between you and your God, and your sins have hidden His face from you so that He does not hear."* <u>Isaiah 59:2</u>

- Doing good works will not make up for your sins. Many people look at it like it is a balance, and they try to do more good deeds to outweigh their bad deeds.
    - *"He saved us, not on the basis of deeds, which we have done in righteousness, but according to His mercy..."* Titus 3:5

- God loves you so much that He gave His only son to die for your sins!
    - *"But God demonstrates His own love toward us, in that while we were yet sinners, Christ died for us."* Romans 5:8
    - *"For God so loved the world that He gave His only begotten Son, that whoever believes in Him shall not perish, but have eternal life."* John 3:16

- There are only two paths in life. One is to follow God. The other is to follow Satan. There is no comfortable middle ground, as many think there is. So if you are not following after God, you are automatically following after Satan and his ways. God's path through Jesus Christ leads us to eternal life in Heaven. Satan's path leads us to eternal life in Hell.
    - *"For the wages of sin is death, but the gift of God is eternal life in Jesus Christ our Lord."* Romans 6:23

- How does one receive this salvation?
    - You must seek after God with your whole heart.
        - *"You will seek Me and find Me when you search for Me with all your heart.* Jeremiah 29:13

    - Jesus tells us that we need to Repent!
        - *From that time Jesus began to preach and say, "Repent, for the kingdom of heaven is at hand."* Matthew 4:17

    - Paul in Romans says: *"...if you confess with your mouth Jesus as Lord and believe in your heart that*

God raised Him from the dead, you will be saved; for with the heart a person believes, resulting in righteousness, and with the mouth he confesses, resulting in salvation." Romans 10:9-10

Note: If it is your sincere desire to receive Jesus into your heart as your personal Lord and Savior, then see Appendix: *Salvation in Three Parts.*

Appendix: <u>TEST LEVEL 1</u>

1.   Name the 3 parts of mankind.

2.   Name the 3 parts of the soul.

3.   What part of us can the enemy not touch?

4.   Where is a stronghold located?

5.   What are 3 ways strongholds can be formed?

6.   What are the first two important steps in conquering strongholds once they have been identified?

7.   What is a soul tie?

8.   What are the 2 kinds of soul ties?

9.   How much time do we give ourselves before we MUST forgive?

10.   What are the 3 steps to forgiving someone once that time is up?

11.   Can Christians have demons?

12.   How much do you really believe that? (Scale of 0% to 100%)

13.   What is one of the most important but often forgotten steps of salvation?

14.   Most demons have how many functions?

15.   Do we do deliverance on non-Christians? Why or why not?

16.   What are 5 possible ways we can tell if there is a demonic presence near us?

17. What are 5 stronghold items we should remove from our homes?

18. What is generational iniquity?

19. <u>Matthew 6:14-15</u> If we do not _____ neither will our Father In Heaven_____

20. <u>Proverbs 18:21</u> _____ and _____ are in the power of the tongue.

Appendix: TEST LEVEL 1 ANSWERS

1. Body, Soul, Spirit
2. Mind, Will, Emotions
3. Spirit
4. Soul
5. Wounding, Sin, Generational Iniquities
6. Asking the Lord to take back the ground from the enemy and break the stronghold from the soul.
7. A soul tie is a linkage in the spiritual realm between two people. Soul ties can be good (e.g. in marriage) or they can be bad (e.g. fornication, adultery, etc.).
8. Sexual and non-sexual
9. Until the sun goes down, or 24 hours max
10. Pray the *Prayer to Grant Forgiveness.*
    Release the person to God.
    Cease thinking about it.
11. Yes!
12. In time as you work with deliverance, your answer will be 100% ☺
13. Repentance!
14. One
15. No, because if the stronghold is not broken, the demons could come back 7 times worse
16. Answers will vary: Chills, fear, contention, headache, nausea, hair standing up on skin, etc.
17. Answers will vary: Religious souvenirs from other countries, certain movies, certain books, music that glorifies Satan in any way (including glorifying or making light of fornication, adultery, abuse of any type, etc.), pornography, etc.
18. Generational iniquity is the iniquity of the forefathers that continues on through the generations because it is "taught" (by word and/or action) by fathers to sons and daughters.
19. Forgive others…Forgive us.
20. Death…Life

WHAT TO EXPECT IN
DELIVERANCE FOR CHRISTIANS LEVEL 2
Weapons of Warfare and Walking It Out

The Level 2 book is intermediate deliverance material that delves into helping us understand more about the ways the enemy can affect lives, and how we can use advanced Spiritual Warfare techniques to help ourselves and others get free. This will also include teaching on how to walk out freedom once one has received it.

TOPICS COVERED

- *Prophetic Dreams and Visions*

- *Places of Captivity: Recognizing and Releasing from Spiritual Captivity*

- *Weapons of Our Warfare (Including some you never thought of as weapons)*

- *More About The Spiritual Realm: Angels and Demons*

- *How to Walk Out Your Freedom in Christ and Avoid Future Bondage*

- *Testimonies of Spiritual Warfare for the Family and City*

Made in the USA
Monee, IL
15 November 2020